Stalking the Wild Amaranth

JANET MARINELLI

DRAWINGS BY STEPHEN K-M. TIM

Stalking the Wild Amaranth

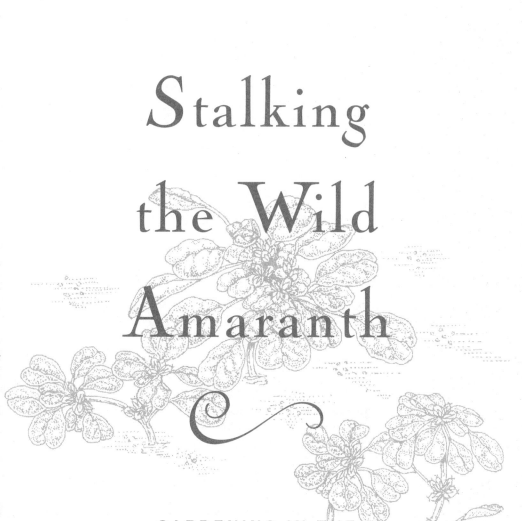

GARDENING IN THE
AGE OF EXTINCTION

HENRY HOLT AND COMPANY / NEW YORK

HENRY HOLT AND COMPANY, INC.
Publishers since 1866
115 West 18th Street
New York, New York 10011

Portions of a few chapters in this book were first published in various
Brooklyn Botanic Garden publications. Parts of the section on invasive
plants appeared in *Restoration & Management Notes* 13, no. 2 (1995).

Library of Congress Cataloging-in-Publication Data

Marinelli, Janet.
Stalking the wild amaranth : a gardener's odyssey in the age of extinction / Janet
Marinelli ; drawings by Stephen K-M. Tim.—1st ed.
p.   cm.
Includes bibliographical references (p.   ) and index.
ISBN 0-8050-4415-9 (hb)
1. Gardening—Philosophy.   2. Garden ecology.   3. Natural gardens, American.
4. Marinelli, Janet.   I. Title.
SB454.3.P45M37   1998
635'.01'577—dc21   97-27538

Henry Holt books are available for special promotions and premiums.
For details contact: Director, Special Markets.

FIRST EDITION 1998

Designed by Gretchen Achilles

Printed in the United States of America
All first editions are printed on acid-free paper. ∞

1   3   5   7   9   10   8   6   4   2

To Don

Contents

Stalking
the Wild
Amaranth

Introduction:
Stalking the Wild Amaranth

MY LEGS WERE killing me; I was ready to collapse in the sand and take a nap. Only sheer vanity kept me going: no way was I going to wimp out now and make Brooklyn Botanic Garden botanist Steve Clemants rue the day he agreed to let me accompany him on his five-day pursuit of the elusive seabeach amaranth. Feeling the weight of every Milky Way bar I'd devoured over the past twelve months, I plodded on.

It was late September, my second day of combing the ocean beaches of eastern Long Island for this rare wild relative of the showy celosias, amaranths, and gomphrenas that so many gardeners lust after. The day before, Steve and I had trudged thirteen miles through the sand, searching between tide line and dune for the plant, which had for forty years been thought extinct in New York State. Not a trace.

For years I've thought nothing about driving clear across the state in quest of the perfect delphinium for my flower border. But this was the first time I'd ever headed out to hunt for plants of the nongarden persuasion. As the sun arced across the sky and the wind continued to whip my face, I felt a new respect for professional plantwatchers such as Steve.

"Tough life," I'd replied, green with envy, when he first mentioned that he was going to the Hamptons to look for some endangered whatchamacallit. I'd trade my computer for a field guide any day.

Steve and his fellow classical botanists, called taxonomists, see life in terms of genus and species. They're interested in which plants grow where. They wield microscopes and work in laboratories but also get out into the bush. They are the front line in the worldwide effort to save species, sounding the alarm on those that are on the verge of extinction. Some write so-called monographs on particular groups of plants, while others spend lifetimes working on "floras"—basically, catalogs of the vegetation of certain geographic regions.

Taxonomists are as rare as an increasing number of the plants they study. Most young biologists these days are instead attracted to the Nobel-spangled fields of microbiology. If those who investigate the subatomic universe of plant DNA are the celebrities of contemporary botany, then taxonomists must be the grunts—or so I concluded as I nursed a blister on my big toe during one of our all-too-infrequent rest stops.

"What ever made you decide to become a botanist?" I asked dubiously.

"It happened the spring semester of my freshman year," said Steve, an understated Minnesotan with a bushy red beard and the patience of a saint. "I started out as a computer-science major. But I was spending all my days waiting for computer cards to run, playing blackjack in student lounges. One beautiful spring day I decided I'd rather be outdoors."

Thus are great careers born.

"But why *plants?*" I persisted.

"I had a garden. I like plants. And taxonomy is a little like solving puzzles."

"Right: intrepid botanists probing the conundrum of evolution," I groused, gingerly removing clumps of sand from my tattered toe.

"Besides, plants don't bleed. I'd feel guilty if I were going around collecting birds or mammals."

Whereas most American botanists track the devastation of biodiversity in the tropics, Steve is surveying the plant life of one of the largest, densest metropolitan areas on Earth: the five boroughs of New York, plus all counties within fifty miles of the city line. Big cities are the stepchildren of the botanical world. Not surprisingly, most botanists prefer exploring an unspoiled rain forest to mucking around in the Fresh Kills landfill, the Big Apple's premier garbage dump, or diving to the ground at the sound of gunfire, as Steve did one day when he was plant collecting at an abandoned warehouse on the Brooklyn side of the East River. He was convinced he was a goner until he realized that what he was hearing was a tape recording intended to keep pigeons from roosting on the dilapidated structure.

When Henry Hudson landed in Brooklyn, in 1609, he sang the praises of its white ocean strands blanketed with beach plum and prickly pear. Before the hot dogs and the hurly-burly, Coney Island's world-famous beach was backed by wind-blown dunes. Before there was an Ebbet's Field and crowds roared for Jackie Robinson, there was an ancient oak forest here. Before jets roared in and out of Kennedy Airport, southern Brooklyn was one big salt marsh, where herons and egrets flapped over vast expanses of marsh grass and glasswort punctuated by the huge, saucerlike white and rose-colored blooms of the marsh mallow.

Brooklyn lies at the western end of Long Island, a huge heap of rocks and sand deposited by the glaciers that has long loomed large in the imaginations of American poets and writers. "Fish-shape Paumanok," the island's Indian name, appears often in the poems of Walt Whitman, who was born here on May 31, 1819. By Whitman's day, most of the majestic forest of oak and chestnut that once blanketed the island's spine—the great moraine left by the last ice sheet—had already been destroyed. South of the moraine, however, the immense outwash plain of sand and gravel was still largely covered with pitch pine, a continuation of the pine barrens of neighboring New Jersey. Here and there the barrens were interrupted by impenetrable thickets of dwarf oak, scarcely more than a foot high.

At the very eastern extremity of the island, a little more than a hundred miles from the first Dutch settlements in Brooklyn, the isolated promontory jutting out into the Atlantic remained essentially wilderness as late as the 1920s, when Norman Taylor observed in *Brooklyn Botanic Garden Memoirs* that "casual visitors to Montauk"—as the promontory has been known since earliest times—"are charmed by the place, the desolate moor-like downs, the depths of the kettleholes, some destitute of woody vegetation, others dark and even mysterious in their wooded interior."

Long Island has certainly loomed large in my own mind. I was born here, and over the past few decades I've watched New York City sprawl relentlessly eastward, all the way to Montauk, where Steve and I now trekked by some of the world's most spectacular beach houses in search of one of the world's rarest plants.

Long Island's mosaic of native plant communities has also been transformed by several centuries of plant immigrants brought here by human settlers from their former homelands. Some of these plants arrived as stowaway seed, hiding in ship ballast dumped along the Brooklyn waterfront, or clinging to the bottoms of people's shoes; others were brought on purpose. *Ailanthus altissima*, for example—the tree-of-heaven immortalized in the book *A Tree Grows in Brooklyn*—was introduced as a garden plant in 1784; today, ecologists might call it the tree-from-hell. Able to sprout even from cracks in pavement, it has become a noxious weed from coast to coast.

Scientists who study the flora of metropolitan areas are engaged in a kind of detective work, surveying species that have naturalized in parks and on roadsides, scrutinizing old herbarium specimens, and scouring historical documents, old photos, and period paintings for evidence of the area's former plant life. With each additional clue, they are better able to determine what has become of the oldtimers, and what the newcomers have wrought. Ultimately, this will tell us a good deal about the future of life on this rapidly urbanizing planet.

For seabeach amaranth, at least, the future looks bleak. An annual plant in the Amaranthaceae (amaranth family), it was first recorded by European botanist Constantine Samuel Rafinesque, who collected a specimen on the Jersey shore in 1803 or 1804. The plant was noted repeatedly by botanists over the next 110 years, but while in 1889 Nathaniel Lord Britton, in a catalog of the plants of New Jersey, could describe seabeach amaranth as being "frequent . . . on sandy sea-beaches," only twenty-two years later, in 1911, Witmer Stone would list it as "apparently local and not common." The last record of seabeach amaranth in New Jersey came just two years later, in 1913. In a period of less than thirty years, the plant had gone from "frequent" to "not common" to extirpated.

Seabeach amaranth is endemic to the beaches of Atlantic Coast barrier islands; it occurs nowhere else in the world. Once found on beaches from Rhode Island to South Carolina, by 1989 it had been reduced to a handful of populations on the Carolina coast. Today, seabeach amaranth has a global conservation-priority ranking of "G2," meaning that it is imperiled throughout its range, with few individuals remaining.

Seabeach amaranth (Amaranthus pumilus),
showing the utricles containing its seaworthy
seeds in the foreground.

This trend is difficult to fathom, if only because seabeach amaranth is one spunky plant. It grows on the upper strands of noneroding beach, that precarious space between tide line and foredune. There it germinates in pure sand. No other vascular plant ventures closer to the ocean.

Seabeach amaranth is supremely adapted to its rough-and-tumble habitat. Its seeds are encased in, but do not quite fill, a pointed bladder called a utricle; because space is left for air, utricles can float in water for a day or so. Both the seed and the utricle itself have a water-repellent, waxy coating. Utricles can also be easily blown about by the wind, skipping rapidly along the surface of the sand.

What the plant apparently can't tolerate is a beach's functioning in anything other than a natural and dynamic manner. This seaside annual must be able to move around in the landscape like a fugitive species, occupying whatever suitable habitat is available. For this reason, beach erosion and most attempts to curtail it—bulkheads, seawalls, jetties, riprap, and even sand fences and dune revegetation—have meant the death of seabeach amaranth. According to the U.S. Fish and Wildlife Service draft recovery plan for the species, it is no coincidence that seabeach amaranth disappeared first from New Jersey, where shoreline stabilization has been going on since the latter part of the nineteenth century. The beachfront houses and condos that today form a new kind of unbroken wall along vast stretches of the coast have further fragmented what little habitat remains: surviving patches of suitable habitat now tend to be too far apart for even the ingeniously adapted seeds of seabeach amaranth to travel, and little recolonization is possible.

While biologists have long suspected that the ever-increasing reach of human society has taken its toll on native plant life, a lack of detailed historical data has left them unable to calculate precisely the extent of the damage. The story of seabeach amaranth provides a discrete piece of evidence. A ground-breaking study published in 1993 in the *Bulletin of the Torrey Botanical Club* offers the first extensive look at the fate of native species in the wake of urban development.

Three biologists at Rutgers University—George Robinson, Mary Yurlina, and Steven Handel—analyzed an unusual series of plant inventories kept over a period of 112 years on Staten Island. Like adjacent Long Island, this seventy-square-mile borough of New York City sits astride an urban corridor that has the highest population density in the United States. The Rutgers scientists found that since 1879, Staten Island's native flora has been drastically reduced, with more than 40 percent of the species once cataloged now missing. Nonnative species have meanwhile become an increasingly dominant part of the island's plant life, increasing from 19 to 33 percent of the total flora. Even on Staten Island, where there is still much that is green and where 10 percent of the land is protected, no type of plant, whether delicate orchid or tenacious tree, has been spared. Plants from every type of habitat, from wetland to woodland, have been affected.

As a borough of New York City, Staten Island is unique in that urban and suburban development has only recently begun to match that seen in other areas of the city or in nearby northeastern New Jersey. In 1931 the island had a population of 160,000; over the past few decades, that number has ballooned to approximately 400,000. If atypical of the region, Staten Island's intense urbanization in recent years is nonetheless typical of a worldwide pattern. The twentieth century has witnessed a profound change in human living arrangements: whereas as late as 1900, only forty-three cities in the world had populations exceeding 500,000, and another sixteen had populations of over one million, now some 400 cities count more than one million inhabitants. Sprawling metropolitan areas have become the norm in nations with advanced economies, and in some instances, even larger agglomerations, with populations in the tens of millions—such as the Boston-to-Washington megalopolis, of which metropolitan New York is the heart—have emerged. Urbanization is experiencing its quickest rise in species-rich Latin America, Africa, and South Asia. The decades-long migration from farm to city accounts for only about a third of the ongoing urban explosion; the Earth's swelling human population is responsible for the rest.

IN 1387 OR thereabouts, Chaucer wrote the *Canterbury Tales*, a fictitious account of a band of twenty-odd pilgrims on their way to the shrine of the English saint Thomas à Becket, the archbishop of Canterbury. This cycle was Chaucer's way of telling the story, from a medieval Christian's point of view, of humanity's brief passage through life to celestial paradise. Several centuries later, Colombus and other Renaissance explorers would journey around the world in search of the Garden of Eden, which was assumed still to exist. Here in the new land they discovered, gardeners have since struggled, like those on other continents before us, to re-create a bit of paradise in an often baffling and unpredictable world. Europe during the Middle Ages had walled gardens, places of refuge from the sinful world. The sixteenth century saw the cultivation of splendid formal gardens with exquisitely sheared shrubs, knotted hedges, and perfect symmetry, while France's eighteenth-century monarchy, the representatives of God on Earth, gave us the florid geometry of Versailles. We Americans seek a similar reassurance from our expanses of emerald-green lawn and our gas barbecues.

For centuries our gardens, with their intimations of order, gave us hope. Now, however, in the waning years of the twentieth century, our capacity to impose our own will on nature is a source as much of consternation as of comfort. And so we scour the far reaches of the planet for plants and animals on the brink of extinction, in a kind of melancholy quest for ecological redemption. At least that's why *I* was in the Hamptons. After years of immersing myself in the cultivated comfort of my own gardens, I found myself gravitating, more and more, to seabeach amaranth and the other waifs and wastrels of the plant kingdom.

Scientists have explored the physical world from the nuclei of atoms to the expanses of far-flung galaxies, yet the domain of living things on Earth remains terra incognita, a realm so unexplored that biologists, in the words of Harvard entomologist and author Edward O. Wilson, "are close to traveling blind." Yet as we chop down, plow up, and urbanize the Earth's ecosystems, we are consigning species to oblivion.

We are poised on the brink of an age of extinction, a biological disaster that could rival anything in evolutionary history, including the mass extinction of the dinosaurs some sixty-five million years ago. Although it has been interrupted on a number of occasions by periods of extinction—five of them episodes of "mass extinction"—the increase in the diversity and complexity of species since life began nearly four billion years ago is astonishing.

Scientists have yet to agree about the extent of current biological losses. Some believe they are a continuation of what Ross MacPhee, chairman of the Department of Mammalogy at the American Museum of Natural History, has called the "40,000-year plague of human-induced extinctions" ushered in during the final phase of the Pleistocene Age, when woolly rhinos, mastodons, cave bears, and other large mammals in the Americas and Australia were extirpated as humans moved into these continents. Other scientists suggest that extinctions occur in pulses—perhaps because thresholds are passed for different organisms at different times—and that a new wave of extermination caused by humans is about to begin.

The *Global Biodiversity Assessment*, a weighty tome that

includes the work of about fifteen hundred scientific experts from around the world, provides the most comprehensive picture to date of Earth's biological diversity and the threats to it. After enumerating the uncertainties surrounding any attempt to compare current extinction rates with rates calculated from the fossil record, the editors conclude, "It is obvious that the rate of extinction today is hundreds, if not thousands, of times higher than the natural background rate that prevailed before the beginning of rapid human population growth a few thousand years ago." There is almost universal agreement that if human population growth continues on its present course, current extirpation rates will accelerate into massive spasms of extinction in the decades to come.

Contrary to popular belief, this threat to biodiversity is occurring not just in the tropical rain forests, though the largest number of species is there. It's also happening here at home. From the Amazonian jungles to the glamorous beaches of Long Island, scientists are already fighting the brushfires of extinction.

As wilderness shrinks and backyard acreage increases, the home gardener's role in this biological debacle grows ever greater. Across a continent of breathtaking biological diversity, we have planted two or three dozen plants. It's no wonder that botanists consider one third of this country's native plants to be anywhere from rare to critically imperiled—and these are plants that provide critical habitat for countless other creatures.

The loss of species may not be the most significant threat to the complexity of life on this otherwise undistinguished orb as it hurtles through space with countless and, so far as we know, lifeless other planets. Threats to genetic and ecosystem diversity are of equal or possibly even greater importance. "Whatever the uncertainties may be about the scale of extinctions," according to *Global Biodiversity Assessment*, "what is clear is that many species will be reduced to small and fragmented populations in the near future." It is just such successive local extirpations—like those of seabeach amaranth—that precipitate a species's slide from common to rare to endangered to extinct.

"Janet! Come here!" All of a sudden, Steve was waving furiously. I limped over as fast as I could. Steve, normally not the most emotional kind of guy, was beaming. There it was: *Amaranthus pumilus*, a little mound of a plant about a foot across, with fleshy reddish stems and small, spinach-green leaves clustered at the tips of the branches. The kind of plant most of us gardeners would gladly yank out of our flowerbeds. But charming nonetheless.

Seabeach amaranth, after not being seen in New York or most of the other states in its historical range for decades, had joined the ranks of plants waiting in the long queue to be listed as official U.S. endangered species. Then, out of the blue, it had been spotted on Long Island in the summer of 1990—and not just one plant, but thirteen distinct populations! Nobody knows why, or how, it returned. One guess is that its seaworthy seed was washed ashore by Hurricane Hugo, which had lashed the Atlantic Coast from the Carolinas to Cape Cod the year before.

Steve was snapping away with his camera. I was thrilled, too. It was like the first time I saw a shy, well-camouflaged—and very imperiled—piping plover scurrying along the beach. One big difference between the two is that birds, when threatened, can fly away; rooted in place, plants are necessarily much more vulnerable. Sometime since the last high tide, our amaranth, one of the rarest creatures in the world, had been squashed by a four-wheel-drive vehicle.

Although I pride myself on my gardening prowess and knowledge of plants, I can't tell you how many times I'd walked the beaches of Long Island without the slightest clue that they harbored the rarest of amaranths, or that the plant itself had been missing from the island's shores for my entire lifetime and then, mysteriously, had returned. It's not as if I knew nothing about the amaranths, a family of some sixty-five genera and nine hundred species around the world. This remarkable botanical clan includes not only a handful of horticultural celebrities but also a couple of important grains that have their own brutal history, and that in fact may have been among the earliest domesticated plants.

Any gardener worth his salt is familiar with the cascading pinkish-red tassels of love-lies-bleeding (*Amaranthus caudatus*), the bizarre bright-red and yellow cockscomb (*Celosia cristata*), the vibrant magenta spheres of globe amaranth (*Gomphrena globosa*), and the trunk-shaped blooms of elephant's head (*Amaranthus tricolor* var. *gangeticus*). These beauties, some of the most distinctive in the plant kingdom, were beloved by turn-of-the-century gardeners. Like everything Victorian, they subsequently fell out of favor, but they're now on the rebound again after decades of horticultural exile. Likewise, grain amaranth (*Amaranthus hypochondriacus*) is one of the trendiest items in health-food stores and in the gardens of the cognoscenti.

Less than five hundred years ago, growing grain amaranth could cost a gardener his or her life. When Cortés landed his armada of eleven Spanish ships at the Gulf Coast port of Veracruz in 1519, he encountered the Aztecs, members of an advanced agricultural civilization that valued *Amaranthus hypochondriacus* as the most important plant cultivated in its sophisticated floating gardens. In his zeal to subdue the Aztecs, Cortés ordered the mass destruction of this staple crop, along with the execution of anyone who tried to grow it.

Because the small, ivory-colored seeds of grain amaranth contain more protein than other grains and cereals, they offer great potential as a food crop in a world in which the biodiversity of edible plants is shrinking fast. Whereas in the mid–nineteenth century there were about four dozen staple crops around the world, today humanity is dependent on no more

Grain amaranth
(Amaranthus hypochondriacus).

than twelve: corn, wheat, barley, soybeans, potatoes, rice, millet, sorghum, oats, rye, peas, and peanuts. Grain amaranth has recently become the focus of efforts to diversify our food supply.

Amaranthus pumilus, though devoid of nutritional and horticultural virtues, has the largest seed in the genus and could prove immensely useful to hybridizers—that is, if it isn't extirpated first. Seabeach amaranth is now gone from six of the nine states in which it once grew. In New York, only four of the thirteen populations that serendipitously reappeared after Hurricane Hugo survive, and two of these populations consist of a single plant. The species also appears to be vulnerable in South Carolina, where only a precious few viable populations of over a hundred plants remain. The national seashores of North Carolina are the final stronghold of this gravely threatened plant.

To be honest, I threw in that item about seed size halfheartedly. There are those who insist that we humans won't give a hoot about saving endangered species unless and until we're given some practical (meaning, human-centered) reason to do so. You've heard the arguments, I'm sure: save the rain forest because no one knows how many cures for cancer are there just waiting to be discovered. Eat Rainforest Crunch, the sweet concoction made of nuts harvested from the moist tropics, because your doing so will increase the value of these beleaguered habitats, and valuable habitats are less likely to be destroyed. Yes, on some intellectual level I understand this train of thought. But I must confess that it was a gut-level feeling that compelled me to join the search for seabeach amaranth, a deep-down-inside discomfort about the fact that our activities, including our seemingly innocuous puttering around the garden, have caused so many species to have such a tenuous lease on existence—a discomfort that has intensified with the continuing discovery on the frontiers of science that all the creatures that inhabit this planet share the same genetic material, albeit arranged in different forms. Whereas classical biologists have emphasized the differences among various organisms, microbiologists unlocking the genetic code tend to see the commonality of life forms. What their work tells me is that deep in our genes, *Amaranthus pumilus* and I are kin.

It was this increasing discomfort that was driving me out of my garden and into the field, library, and lab to answer some basic questions. Will we destroy seabeach amaranth and other plants as surely, if not as deliberately, as Cortés eradicated the grain amaranth? What is a gardener to do in a biologically homogenizing world? If we put our minds to it, can we gardeners, with our centuries of practical experience in growing plants, help rescue species from the brink of extinction and restore ancient natural communities that have become more and more fragmented and degraded? What *is* our role, as the quintessential self-conscious species, in the greater destiny of the Earth? This book is my humble attempt to sort it all out.

Garden Place

e⌒

I GREW UP on Long Island, on a block called Garden Place. It sounds like a perfect name for a horticultural soap opera. Politically, it could have been scripted by Thomas Jefferson; ecologically, by Stephen King.

Grandma grew tomatoes. Dad mowed the lawn. Every Mother's Day, Mom got another pink azalea or the latest shade of creeping phlox. Today my childhood home looks like just about every other suburban garden between Boston and Seattle, with its golf-course-quality lawn, clipped yews, azaleas, and shade trees ringed by inner tubes of impatiens.

Suburbia has been called the quintessential physical achievement of the United States. "Suburbia symbolizes the fullest, most unadulterated embodiment of contemporary culture," writes Kenneth Jackson in his classic study *Crabgrass Frontier*. It has become quite trendy, especially among baby-boomer garden writers like me, to poke fun at the suburban landscape. I have a hopelessly love-hate relationship with suburbia: one minute I'm getting all misty-eyed over the gardens of my youth, and the next I'm convinced that they're evil incarnate.

Some writers have made much of the fact that the suburban yard, particularly the lawn, is a throwback, a garden idea ripped off from eighteenth-century England—just another piece of evidence in the argument that as far as landscaping goes, America is in the little leagues compared to the British Isles. In the 1700s, English landscapers threw off the yoke of the French formal garden, with its raised beds of grass shaped in ornate patterns. Inspired partly by paintings that invoked classical images of Arcadia, where humans supposedly lived in harmony with nature, they engineered new, naturalistic landscapes, using lawn to blend the estates of the English gentry into the surrounding countryside, thus creating the illusion that the cultivated flowed seamlessly into the wild.

Capability Brown and the other masters of the English landscape garden pulled off this trick by hiring armies of workers to contour the land into perfectly smooth surfaces on which expansive lawns could be planted. In the process, they destroyed ancient yew hedges, razed gracious old avenues of trees, dismantled houses, and displaced entire villages.

These innovators and their inventions made quite an impression. The English landscape garden formed the vanguard of an intellectual revolution that to this day continues to influence the way we perceive nature and our place in it. It also cemented the lawn as the great status symbol of late-eighteenth-century British society—a status symbol that was promptly transplanted to the New World, where it has proved even more enduring.

Thomas Jefferson was particularly enamored of the English landscape garden. In his journal, Jefferson noted that the lawn of one Brownian landscape, Moor Park, measured "about thirty acres." The British model could be easily adapted to his vision of an American democracy founded upon and made up of citizen farmers, each working his own land. The view from the flowing lawn at Jefferson's home, Monticello, led through a working farm landscape before ending in wild nature. The new pastoral landscape of lawns would link the citizens of a democracy not only to nature and thereby to each other, but also to the rarefied world of higher learning. The original campus of my own alma mater, the University of Virginia, which Jefferson created for the education of the new nation's citizen farmers, was called, tellingly, The Lawn. Here, a string of classically inspired buildings are arranged in the shape of a U around an elegant tiered expanse of turf.

By the mid–nineteenth century, the Americanization of the English landscape garden had passed squarely into the hands of the middle class. The objective was no longer a working farm gussied up with the requisite turf, however, but rather a suburban single-family home surrounded by lawn. "Probably the advantages of civilization can be found illustrated and demonstrated under no other circumstances so completely as in some suburban neighborhoods where each family abode stands fifty or a hundred feet or more apart from all others, and at some distance from the public road," Frederick Law Olmsted wrote at this time. The necklace of lawn encircling each abode, he believed, unified a neighborhood both aesthetically and politically.

So Americans borrowed the lawn from the British—so what? In less than a century, we transformed their aristocratic turf into an ingenious expression of egalitarian ideals, with all those unfenced patches of suburban front lawn uniting us as a democracy and as a people.

Now, that's a nice thought. But the reality is that the popularity of the suburban landscape is owed less to political philosophers such as Jefferson than to nineteenth-century proponents of what today are called "family values," proponents like Catharine Beecher, a kind of Victorian cross between Phyllis Schlafly and Martha Stewart.

Catharine Beecher was born into a family in which, it has been noted, the "missionary fires burned brightly." Among her seven brothers, all of them ministers, was Henry Ward Beecher, the leading Protestant clergyman of the mid–nineteenth century. Catharine's sister Harriet Beecher Stowe was the author of *Uncle Tom's Cabin*, the novel that helped start the Civil War. Another sister, Isabella, was one of the foremost feminists of her day.

Catharine never had her own home and family, and reportedly was rarely on friendly terms with her relatives. But that didn't stop her from publishing twenty-five books fleshing out her vision of a healthy, happy, well-fed family living harmoniously in a well-constructed, well-appointed, and well-kept house. Beecher's *Treatise on Domestic Economy, For the Use of Young Ladies at Home and at School* first appeared in 1841 and was reprinted dozens of times over the next thirty years.

Beecher believed that family life could best thrive in a semi-rural, suburban setting. A full five chapters of her *Treatise* were devoted to the garden, for she considered "healthful outdoor occupation in the family service," as she put it, to be of primary importance. Nothing escaped her notice; she had opinions on everything from the rearing of children to the correct placement of the indoor privy. To Beecher, the universe was divided into the female-dominated sphere of home life (preferably suburban) and the male-dominated (and usually urban) business world. It was up to the ladies, the morally superior but subservient sex, to keep the home pious and pure through proper house and garden design.

Forget those noble ideals of Jeffersonian democracy; don't listen to the analysts who blame suburbia on the automobile. Thanks to Catherine Beecher, the suburban boom in America has gone hand in hand with the baby boom. The same irresistible urge that led Beecher's contemporaries from the Bronx to Bronxville led my parents from Brooklyn to the wilds of Long Island in the 1950s. It continues to cast its spell to this day: virtually all the pregnant women I know—even formerly vociferous urbanites—begin combing the real estate ads for a house in the suburbs before they even go for their first sonogram.

The post–World War II Long Island where I grew up was fertile ground for this century's great twist in the suburban spiral. Long Island was the site of America's first concrete nonstop automobile road, the Vanderbilt Motor Parkway, which ran from the Queens border to Lake Ronkonkoma, a deep ditch scoured out by the last glacier. Built in 1908, the parkway was the forerunner of the modern superhighway. The nation's first supermarket, King Kullen, was established on Long Island in 1930, and its first true subdivision, Levittown, followed inexorably in 1946, when Abraham Levitt and his two sons began acquiring four thousand acres of potato farm smack in the middle of Nassau County. There they built the biggest private housing project in American history, which enabled young couples like my mom and dad, squashed in with their in-laws or crammed into tiny apartments in the city, to afford their own pastoral dreams.

The modest Cape Cod house on a quarter acre of land that my parents purchased some forty-six years ago is not far from Levittown, on the edge of what was once the largest prairie on the East Coast. Called the Hempstead Plain, the treeless area covered about sixty thousand acres. A hard turf of little bluestem grass was tinged purple in early spring when the bird's-foot violet bloomed. Clumps of wild indigo and dwarf willow stood out as knoblike projections on these plains. An early settler wrote that "cattle lying down in the grass were lost to sight" and warned that a "man might miss his way in the tall grass."

This wild landscape has been transformed into a sprawling mosaic of utterly feminine domestic landscapes, in which each plant is treasured like some precocious toddler or cranky elder member of the family. The June rose that once climbed up the side of my parents' garage, delighting us with its bright-red blooms, is gone now, as are all of the original builder's bushes, except for one tenacious old arborvitae. Now about thirty feet tall, it has housed generations of cardinals' nests. All of the greenery on either side of the arborvitae came from one small cutting that Grandma took from a euonymus bush in Aunt Lucy's and Uncle Tommy's yard in nearby Seaford. Today, the euonymus completely obscures the back fence.

Our vegetable garden once occupied the back half of the property. This was Grandma's domain, where she'd be found most every day from spring to fall. The vegetable garden has shrunk to a small patch behind the garage since Grandma died, in 1973. Fig trees are lined up behind the garage, too. We call them Memorial Row. They came from cuttings from both grandmas and from Uncle Nick—all three of them gone now. My mom and dad harvest a bumper crop of figs into late September, then wrap the trees up snug for the winter.

The huge maple tree that my brother, George, and I climbed as kids was struck by lightning one year. The lightning ricocheted off the tree and singed the fringe on our hammock. The tree did not survive, but an oak tree sprouted on almost the same spot, thanks to a squirrel who planted an acorn there. George is gone now, too, but the azalea bushes he gave Mom every Mother's Day still light up the front of the house in DayGlo pinks and reds—as colorful as his personality—each year in May.

One of the most captivating plants in my childhood garden is a peegee hydrangea, which we call the sheepshead, after the shape of its showy, large, long-lasting inflorescences, which open white and become pinkish before turning bronze as winter approaches. Dried sheepsheads gathered from it have decorated the homes of friends and relatives for decades, but the most memorable thing about this venerable bush is the way its gnarled old branches have become twisted and intertwined, giving rise each year to slender new stems that droop from the weight of a new crop of flowers. Kind of like the branches of a family tree.

Sheepshead
(Hydrangea paniculata 'Grandiflora').

IT'S HARD TO fall in love with a grass plant, especially when its identity has been subsumed in a lawn, that horticultural equivalent of a Stalinist collective. So why is it grass that has become the official symbol of suburbia, the heart of the American view of the ideal life? Not the kitchen garden, as in Italy. Not the flower border, as in England. Turfgrass. Go figure.

My husband, Don, rolls his eyes toward the heavens whenever I wax eloquent about how perfect *Juncus effusus* 'Spiralis', a form of the common soft rush with a severely twisted attitude, would be in the wetland border at our Shelter Island summer house. But when we pull up the driveway, the car can barely sputter to a halt before he's off and running to the shed for the rickety reel mower we use to trim the patch of lawn behind the porch (don't tell Don, but it's mostly moss, barren strawberry, and plantain). Mowing the lawn is Don's idea of gardening. After years of meticulous observation, I've concluded that mowing is a guy thing. American men gravitate to turfgrass like slugs to stale beer.

I think it has something to do with all the gizmos: even in the early days, lawn care involved an arsenal of tools. Those Capability Brown landscapes with sheep grazing peacefully on princely greenswards thrived only if they were scythed, brushed, swept, and rolled around the clock to smooth out any imperfections. Englishman Edwin Budding's invention of the lawn mower in 1830 brought lawn within reach of the common man. Today edgers, spreaders, aerators, rollers, weed whackers, mowers from reel to rotary to four-wheel-drive rider models, dusters and sprayers, precision seeders, leaf blowers, hoses, sprinklers, and other irrigation devices, not to mention grass seed specially designed for sun, shade, or both, fertilizers in various formulations, insecticides, herbicides, and fungicides, are among the paraphernalia found in the average suburban garage.

I've watched otherwise perfectly lovable, rational men like my dad go to insane lengths to minister to their lawns. One sweltering summer day about thirty years ago, my father, fed up with our browned-out, mangy-looking lawn, got out the sprayer and *painted* it green—not typical suburban behavior, to be sure, but not entirely out of line, either, with other steps we routinely take in our gardens, especially on our lawns, to get nature to do what it does not want to do.

According to the National Gardening Association, fifty-eight million homeowners around the country rev up their mowers week after week, each spending some forty hours a year to keep the turfgrass gulag under control. Lawn order is preserved by thwarting the grass's sex drive. Instead of treating the grass like a normal plant and encouraging flowers, fruit, and seeds to be set, the typical suburbanite performs weekly castrations. Between mowings, he (and to press the point, it is almost invariably a *he*) waters the lawn like crazy and, several liberally applied times a season, force-feeds it with chemical fertilizers, trying to stimulate the same poor plants to grow, grow, grow.

Our landscaping problems go way beyond this curious routine of horticultural S and M, however. In a natural ecosystem, the sun provides all the energy needed by the resident plants and animals, and drives the water and nutrient cycles that keep them alive. A natural prairie, say, does not require outside intervention because all the native organisms are adapted to the site's conditions. They make do with whatever water comes from natural precipitation and with whatever nutrients are kept constantly cycling between the living and nonliving members of the biological community. In other words, a prairie is solar-powered and fertilizes itself.

Compare this with what goes on in that human-modified grassland ecosystem, the lawn. To achieve the requisite perfectly manicured look, lawn clippings are often removed and carted off to the nearest landfill. Fertilizers are then applied to replace the lost nutrients. Fertilizer production is entirely dependent on fossil fuels, particularly natural gas, stored underground for millions of years since the dinosaur era, often half a world away. Gasoline derived from crude oil fuels most power mowers.

In many areas, the lawn is irrigated with fossil water deposited in underground aquifers thousands of years ago by glaciers. Over the past forty years, for example, about thirteen hundred *trillion* gallons have been withdrawn from the Ogallala Aquifer, which stretches from South Dakota to northern Texas. Because this is far more water than is being replaced by natural processes, water tables in these areas are plummeting. In regions that depend on surface water for irrigation, the streamflow in many river basins is decreasing. The National Xeriscape Council, which promotes water-conserving landscaping, estimates that up to 30 percent of urban water on the East Coast is used for lawn irrigation, and up to 60 percent in the arid West.

Meanwhile, insects and fungi view the suburban lawn as the "centerpiece of a huge Bacchanalian feast," in the words of F. Herbert Bormann, Diana Balmori, and Gordon Geballe, the authors of *Redesigning the American Lawn*. Foiling these critters has spawned still another lawn-care industry: pesticide manufacturing. The National Academy of Science has found that homeowners use up to ten times more chemical pesticides than farmers do. These poisons don't kill just the estimated 1 percent of all plant and animal species that are considered pests; they also demolish myriad other creatures in the food chain that perform such essential functions as decomposing wastes and recycling nutrients. To compensate, even more fertilizers and pesticides are needed to keep the lawn healthy.

At the very beginning of their study of the environmental costs of what they call the "industrial lawn," Balmori, Geballe, and Bormann (one of the leading ecologists of the late twentieth century) pose the following questions: Does lawn contribute to global ecological stability or instability? In designing and managing our lawns, have we strayed too far from nature's plan? They conclude that the suburban lawn is a major drain on natural resources and that it also causes severe ecological side effects.

Some of these side effects occur close to home. Our use of fossil fuels and chemical pesticides and herbicides, for example, affects not only our lawns but also interconnected natural systems such as air and water. On the local and regional level, the use of fossil fuels, whether to make fertilizers or to power the machines we use to groom the grass, contributes to smog and acid rain. Although the emissions from one homeowner's mower may seem trivial, the collective emissions of fifty-eight million mowers constitute a massive amount of air pollution. It's been calculated that the emissions produced annually by lawn equipment in California alone are equivalent to what would be emitted by three and a half million 1991 model automobiles driven sixteen thousand miles apiece.

The natural flow of water seeping into the soil and over the surface of the land carries lawn chemicals into underground water supplies as well as into lakes, rivers, streams, and wetlands. As Bormann and his colleagues point out, unlike naturally occurring ecosystems, which usually retain most of their nutrients, human-managed systems often lose substantial amounts. Some of the fertilizer lavished on the lawn may be lost in drainage water. When these excess nutrients end up in nearby bodies of water, they cause eutrophication, or excessive plant growth, which leads to oxygen-poor conditions that can kill fish and other aquatic life. The excess nutrients can also easily move from the surface of the lawn into the groundwater supply on which millions rely for their drinking water. Nitrate, a form of nitrogen, is the most common groundwater contaminant. High concentrations of nitrate in drinking water can cause birth defects, cancer, and the "blue baby" syndrome, which occurs when the oxygen levels in an infant's blood become dangerously low. Lawn pesticides can also contaminate drinking-water supplies. Detectable levels of pesticides or their breakdown products have been discovered in 10 percent of the wells in community water systems; in a small percentage of these, one or more pesticides exceeded levels deemed safe by health officials. The long-term effects on human health or wildlife of the toxins contained in many major lawn-care products have not yet been carefully studied.

Yard waste is one of the largest components of the garbage stream, second only to paper, and much of it ends up in already overburdened landfills. Fully three quarters of this waste consists of grass clippings from lawns. Removal of these same grass clippings may result in the loss of up to one hundred pounds of nitrogen—a natural fertilizer—per acre of lawn, per year.

Some of the other implications of the suburban lawn are even more far-reaching. In recent decades, scientists have learned that overuse of fossil fuels on the lawn and elsewhere contributes to the global greenhouse effect, a wonderfully horticultural term for a rather sinister process that, by disrupting the basic atmospheric cycles that have made the Earth habitable for humans and our fellow creatures for millennia, heats up the planet. Scientists have amassed ample evidence that the average global temperature has already risen about one degree Fahrenheit in the last century, compared to a natural change of less than one degree *per millennium* over the last twelve thousand years. Given the massive amounts of greenhouse pollutants we are continuing to pump into the atmosphere, the climate could soon start to change at a rate never before seen in the fossil record. By now, we've all heard the long litany of disasters that could accompany global warming, from the transformation of temperate farmlands into dustbowls to the swamping of coastal cities by melting polar ice caps. Less well known is the prediction that the ranges of many plants would be forced to shift northward at an unprecedented rate to keep pace with changing conditions. Many species would not survive.

In the United States, some twenty-five million acres, or about forty thousand square miles, are covered by turf—more acreage than is given over to any agricultural crop. In the lawn, plant and animal diversity is ruthlessly eliminated; the idea, after all, is grass, and grass alone. Nature rarely puts all its eggs in one basket; the diverse web of life in a natural prairie or forest has built-in redundancy and therefore resiliency. As a radically simplified system, the lawn will be especially vulnerable as we head into a time that will probably be defined by unprecedented shocks to the natural world—a time when we'll need all the redundancy and resiliency we can get.

Aliens, Clones, and
the Origin of Species

EVERYBODY LOVES A good fight. I'm not talking here about sweaty guys in silk shorts duking it out; I mean the clash of ideas waged via computer in the op-ed pages of the papers or the Sunday news magazines.

Gardeners have always been game to indulge in a bit of horticultural mudslinging. In the eighteenth century, tastemakers had had it with the topiary craze that reached its pinnacle during the reign of William and Mary, when virtually anything green was sheared into lollipops, spirals, poodles, or peacocks. The poet Alexander Pope defined topiary as a "monument to perverted taste" and ridiculed ladies whose dream gardens featured "their own effigies in myrtle, or their husbands' in hornbeam." Two centuries later, the horticultural avant-garde was foaming at the mouth about the then wildly popular Victorian flower bedding schemes. In a 1908 *Ladies Home Journal* article entitled "Pimples on Nature's Face," one writer called such plans "stereotyped beds of screaming geraniums." "And if we are spared the owner's initials in party colors, we are fortunate," he added, breaking into a sweat.

The biggest controversy presently raging in American gardening circles concerns native plants. The issue came to a head in an article published in the May 14, 1994, issue of the *New York Times Magazine*, in which author Michael Pollan suggested that the natural-garden movement, and particularly what he termed the "current attack on alien species," were "ideology masquerading as science."

"It's hard to believe," Pollan wrote, "that there is nothing more than scientific concern about invasive species behind the current fashion for natural gardening and native plants in America—not when our national politics are rife with anxieties about immigration and isolationist sentiment." He pointed to a similar outbreak of "native-plant mania" in Nazi Germany, which "saw the rise of a natural-gardening movement founded on nationalistic and racist ideas that were often cloaked in scientific jargon."

I must admit that my initial reaction to Pollan's article was unsuitable for a family audience. As a natural gardener, I didn't exactly warm to the Nazi comparison; as a journalist familiar with the tricks of the trade, I was less than impressed by the way Pollan focused superficially (and rather sensationally) on the politics of the issue, while blithely dismissing the scientific credibility of both ecological restoration and natural landscaping, its domesticated form—all without talking to a single scientist! But after counting to ten (well, maybe a thousand), I had to allow that given our present political climate, Pollan's charges merited some serious consideration.

A few months after Pollan's article appeared, I began organizing a symposium on the role of native plants in the twenty-first-century garden, as part of a joint celebration of the first anniversary of the Brooklyn Botanic Garden's 21st-Century Gardening series of handbooks and the fiftieth anniversary of handbook publishing at the institution. What better way to add my two cents to this imbroglio than to kick off the day's festivities with a native-plants debate?

Joachim Wolschke-Bulmahn, who was then director of studies in landscape architecture at Dumbarton Oaks in Washington, D.C., and who has written extensively on the rise of a natural-gardening movement in Nazi Germany, agreed to participate. To make the case for native plants, I recruited Neil Diboll, a plant ecologist and the president of Prairie Nursery in Westfield, Wisconsin.

In his opening salvo, Wolschke-Bulmahn noted that contemporary ideas about natural-garden design sounded suspiciously like the National Socialist blood-and-soil ideology of early-twentieth-century Germany. Unlike Pollan, however, he was unwilling to draw a close analogy to the enthusiasm for native plants in the United States today, instead declaring that "it is very important, particularly for me as a German historian . . . to be aware of how ideas about nature can be connected with ideas about society. We shouldn't ignore this problem when discussing native plant issues."

For starters, Wolschke-Bulmahn observed that "many who claim authority by referring to nature or native plants do not offer an unequivocal definition of what they mean by native plants." Defining "native" according to political boundaries such as nation or state, he pointed out, had nothing to do with nature or nativeness.

To support his contention that ideas about nature could be linked to ideas about society, Wolschke-Bulmahn cited examples from the Nazi era in Germany, when the exclusive use of natives "became the landscape architect's swastika." Alwyn Seifert, one of the leading landscape architects of that period, had once argued that in German landscapes, "nothing foreign should be added, and nothing native must be left out." In 1941, work began on a so-called Reich landscape law that would have forbidden the use of nonindigenous plants (the war ended before the law was passed). In 1942, German botanists called for a "war of extermination" against a foreign species of impatiens, *Impatiens parviflora*, that was seen as competing with *Impatiens nolitangere*, considered to be native.

Wolschke-Bulmahn's coup de grace was his assertion that some American natural-landscaping pioneers, themselves contemporaries of Seifert and other Nazi garden designers—the only one mentioned by name being Prairie School landscape designer Jens Jensen—had exhibited "similar tendencies toward racist argumentation." He quoted at length from a 1937 article by Jensen entitled "Die Lichtung" (The Clearing), published in the German journal *Die Gardenkunst*. I have no idea whether or not this quote was pulled out of context; however, I do believe it's healthy for us to be aware of the (possible) foibles as well as the virtues of our heroes, and since Jensen is approaching mythic status among many native-plant enthusiasts, I think his words are worth repeating here.

"The Gardens that I created myself," Jenson wrote

> shall, like any landscape design, it doesn't matter where, be in harmony with the landscape environment and the racial characteristics of its inhabitants. They shall express a spirit of America, and therefore shall be free of foreign character as far as possible. The Latin and the Oriental . . . creep more and more over our land, coming from the South, which is settled by Latin people, and also from other centers of mixed masses of immigrants. The Germanic character of our race, of our cities and settlements, [has been] overgrown by foreign character. Latin spirit has spoiled a lot, and still spoils things every day.

It seems to me that we should be cautious before imputing racist motives to anyone. Still, let's just assume, for the sake of argument, that Jensen's social views were less than saintly. That may be reason enough to reevaluate *his* motives for championing the use of native plants, but does it also necessarily cast doubt on the intentions of other pioneering natural landscapers and restoration ecologists of the day? In the absence of any evidence that they, too, used racist arguments to make the case for native plants, I don't think it does. Does Jensen's racially charged language call into question *all* motives for using native plants? Of course not.

Wolschke-Bulmahn wrapped up his opening argument by asserting that while there were many good reasons for growing natives, ranging from aesthetics to the desire to prevent the extinction of plants and wildlife, nonetheless "there is no reason for a native plant doctrine, and for the assumption that only native plants will serve these functions best." In point of fact, though, there are sometimes *very* good reasons for using native plants to prevent extinctions: blue wild lupine, *Lupinus perennis*, for one, is the only host plant for the larvae of the endangered Karner Blue butterfly. And here, I think, is where this critique of landscape restoration begins to fall apart. Wolschke-Bulmahn, like Pollan, dismissed the scientific case for planting natives without even examining it.

In his opening statement, Neil Diboll addressed Wolschke-Bulmahn's question "What is a native plant?" Nativeness, he said, was a function of two factors: location and time. Using these criteria, he defined native plants basically as those found in a particular ecological region approximately 150 to 200 years ago, before new plants were introduced wholesale or old ones massively displaced by European immigrants to this continent. In other words, gardeners who classify as native any plant that grew in America before the arrival of the Europeans have got it wrong: *Aster spectabilis*, for example, a small aster with light-blue

Blue wild lupine (Lupinus perennis), the only host plant for larvae of the endangered Karner Blue butterfly.

flower petals surrounding a central golden disk, may be indigenous to a garden in New Jersey, but not to one in Oregon, Texas, or Florida.

Diboll emphasized that he was not trying to make a case against change in the landscape, and recognized that the "only thing non-changing about nature is that it is ever-changing." The real issues, he said, related to the rate of change and to what type of change was acceptable. Diboll argued that one clearly unacceptable type of change had been wrought by the small percentage of introduced plants that have become invasive and caused "massive ecological destruction." One reason he chose to grow native plants, he explained, was that that way, "I know I'm not going to be introducing a problem species."

Diboll added that another reason for his choice was that he wanted to restore some semblance of the biological diversity that had once existed on his twenty-acre farm, much of which was now an impenetrable thicket of nonnative buckthorn: "I'm an ecologist, and diversity is the ecologist's bias because to us diversity equals health." Diversity, he pointed out, was not one of the Nazis' highest priorities. He likened native plants to the Jews and Gypsies of the Nazi era, and called invasive nonnatives "storm-trooper plants that are blitzkrieging across the landscape" and displacing native plants, driving them if not to extinction then surely to local extirpation. He therefore favored a period of testing before the introduction of any new plant, to reduce the chance of another invasive species. "Should we have an orderly, Ellis Island approach to [plant] immigration," he asked, "or a chaotic, Mariel boat-lift policy?"

This turned out to be the most contentious issue of the ensuing debate. When asked whether he thought any and all plants should be allowed entry by human means into any ecological region, Wolschke-Bulmahn responded yes, because he feared that regulation of new introductions would discourage people from experimenting and innovating with plants. For his part,

Diboll declared that the issue of regulation of potentially invasive plants was a classic example of the conflict between freedom and responsibility. Many gardeners believe that they have the right to grow any plant they want to, and that the government should not interfere with that right, but, wondered Diboll, "is that fair to other people who will then have to deal with the consequences of the small percentage of nonnative plants that will become problems?"

However polarized their positions may seem, both Wolschke-Bulmahn and Diboll are veritable middle-of-the-roaders in this debate. At the one extreme are the environmental misanthropes who believe that we humans are ecological outlaws and that planting any nonnative is a form of environmental treason; at the other end of the spectrum are those who think we're doing creation a favor every time we introduce another plant. One of the latter is J. L. Hudson, a California-based purveyor of plant seeds who has called the current concern over invasive plants "pseudoscience" and those who have raised it "eco-fascists." "The aid we have given species in their movement around the world has served to increase both global and local diversity," Hudson wrote in a recent mail-order catalog. "We have only a brief moment in history when fossil fuels will continue to allow us rapid worldwide travel. Let us use this time wisely to the benefit of all species."

IS THERE ANY hard data behind the rhetoric?

Scientists around the world are concerned about what they see as the global homogenization of plant life caused by the introduction of nonnative plants and the rise of "weedy" organisms supremely adapted to human-dominated landscapes—a sort of botanical version of the homogenization of international cuisine caused by the Big Mac. In my native stomping grounds on Long Island, for example, exquisite orchids such as the small yellow lady's slipper, *Cypripedium parviflorum*, are being replaced by the turfgrass and begonias favored by suburbanites. Extend the turf and begonias from coast to coast, and you'll get some idea of the magnitude of the plant-homogenization problem. If you throw a few invasives such as purple loosestrife into the equation, you'll begin to understand what all the hoopla's about.

Purple loosestrife, *Lythrum salicaria*, a beautiful perennial best known for its showy spikes of purple flowers in summer, was introduced into the northeastern United States in the early 1800s. It has since spread throughout the temperate regions of North America, invading wetland habitats from marshes and wet meadows to riverbanks and the shores of lakes and ponds. Like other invasive organisms, both plant and animal, the Eurasian native forms extensive stands, displacing native vegetation and reducing the availability of food and shelter for wetland wildlife. A new term for this process, "biological pollution," has lately appeared in scientific journals.

How many plant invaders are there? In the course of researching a Brooklyn Botanic Garden handbook on the subject, we tallied the number of species on the two most comprehensive national weed lists currently available: one of plants being reported as problems on the Nature Conservancy's preserves nationwide, and another compiled by the National Association of Exotic Pest Plant Councils, a Washington, D.C.–based umbrella organization of state groups focused on the ecological impact of invasive species. After submitting the combined list to various state weed authorities for their additions and subtractions, we arrived at a total of just over three hundred plants invading natural areas in the forty-nine continental states and the southern Canadian provinces. (We decided not to include Hawaii in our handbook since the plant invaders of the Hawaiian islands could fill an entire volume by themselves.) Many of the three hundred invasives, such as *Artemisia vulgaris*, the aptly named mugwort that takes over abandoned urban lots, arrived on this continent accidentally; others were introduced as livestock forage. According to our calculations, about half were brought here to embellish our backyards. These are substantial numbers, to be sure, but they represent just a tiny fraction of the thousands of plants that have been introduced into this continent in the past few centuries. A much smaller fraction still of native plants are now showing signs of weedy behavior as well, but there is considerable disagreement as to why and what kind of threat they pose.

Managers of natural areas are struggling to control biological invasions and to preserve the pre-Columbian plant communities on their lands so that these areas can serve as the baseline ecosystems we need to gather knowledge about how nature works. At the same time, nurseries continue to sell and gardeners to plant many invasive species. Take tamarisks, for example—tall shrubs that produce lovely plumes of white-to-pink flowers from spring through fall, first imported into the United States as ornamental plants in the early 1800s. Today, several species in the genus *Tamarix* have escaped cultivation in all western states except Washington and North Dakota. They displace native stream-side vegetation, making these habitats more prone to wildfires, and consume so much water that they can dry up desert oases vital to wildlife. Yet they're still routinely touted as great garden plants for the arid West.

Some invasive plants pose direct threats to rare species or habitats. Beach naupaka, *Scaevola sericea*, a salt-tolerant shrub popular with southern Florida landscapers for coastal plantings, forms extensive colonies on sand dunes, competing directly with the native inkberry, *Scaevola plumieri*, which is on the state's list of threatened species. In Michigan, baby's-breath, *Gypsophila paniculata*, the beloved perennial that produces airy, delicate-looking mounds of tiny white flowers, is invading freshwater dune habitat occupied by *Cirsium pitcheri*, commonly known as pitcher's or dune thistle, which is endemic to the Great Lakes. Dune thistle is on both the federal and state lists of threatened species.

James O. Luken, an ecologist, and John W. Thieret, a plant taxonomist, both of Northern Kentucky University, have documented a chronology of events in the 150-year interaction between western plant scientists and another invasive plant, the eastern Asiatic shrub called amur honeysuckle, *Lonicera maackii*. In their article "Amur Honeysuckle: Its Fall from Grace," the two scientists also recount how competing perceptions of the plant have caused resource managers and horticulturists to work at cross purposes. "It would be difficult to exaggerate the weedy potential of this shrub," wrote F. Swink and G. Wilhelm in a report to the Indiana Academy of Science. "It is one of the most beautiful of bush honeysuckles," wrote plantsman W. J. Bean in a book on recommended trees and shrubs.

Amur honeysuckle is a deciduous shrub that can grow up to thirty feet tall in rich soils. It leafs out in early spring, well before native shrubs, and drops its leaves well after theirs have fallen. The leaves are dark green, with a variety of shapes ranging from lance heads to broad ellipses that taper to a slender point. A profusion of white flowers in spring, sometimes tinged with pink, is followed in fall by an abundance of glossy red fruits.

Amur honeysuckle is native to central and northeastern China, Korea, and Japan. According to Luken and Thieret, the shrub seems to have been cultivated in Chinese gardens long before it caught the eye of European plant hunters. The first herbarium specimen was collected by plant explorer Robert Fortune in 1843, most likely from a Chinese garden. The first American record of the plant is in the archives of the New York Botanical Garden, where seeds were received in 1898 from the U.S. Department of Agriculture's Section of Foreign Seed and Plant Introduction, which distributed seeds of this and other species to commercial growers, botanical gardens, and private collectors across the country. By 1931, the shrub was available from at least eight commercial nurseries.

Amur honeysuckle (Lonicera maackii).

The plant's tendency to reproduce and spread was first noted in the mid-1920s by the Morton Arboretum in Lisle, Illinois; reports of naturalized populations began to appear in the late 1950s. In the words of Luken and Thieret, "These initial reports were harbingers of the invasion to come." But this didn't stop the USDA Soil Conservation Service from leading an effort to develop improved cultivars of *Lonicera maackii* from the 1960s to 1984. The new selections were intended for use by property own-ers to stabilize soil erosion and improve wildlife habitat while beautifying the landscape. Plants already naturalized in various parts of the country were selected and propagated for their espe-cially abundant fruit production, as amur honeysuckle's reliable profusion of flowers and fruits endeared it to people and wildlife alike. One of these cultivars, 'Rem Red', known for its spectacu-lar fruit display, remains available today.

Now, less than a century after it was first introduced into North America, amur honeysuckle is growing and reproducing in twenty-four eastern states and in Ontario, with invasion most intensive in Illinois, Indiana, Kentucky, Ohio, Tennessee, and West Virginia. It is capable of colonizing a variety of habitats, from open fields, marshes, and roadsides to shady forests, though it is most successful in full sun. *Lonicera maackii* and related bush honeysuckles such as *L. morrowii* and *L. tatarica* can trans-form prairie into scrub. In forest preserves they can reduce the plant diversity of the ground layer and decrease the density of tree seedlings, with possible long-term implications for tree populations.

Piecing together how problem plants got here is easy; it's deciding what should be done about them that's the hard part. Jim Luken, who has been studying bush honeysuckles for years, points out that few in-depth studies have been undertaken to determine how these shrubs interact with other species in bio-logical communities. Clearly, native birds now feed on the honeysuckles' fruit in winter and may use the shrubs for nesting; and Luken notes that under some circumstances, ripping out dense thickets may be counterproductive because it exposes soil, making it susceptible to erosion or invasion by other aggressive species. In a 1994 article in *Natural Areas Journal*, he raised the eyebrows of many resource managers and weed specialists by suggesting, among other things, that quick and haphazard action to eradicate plant invaders may render an area even less functional ecologically. He also proposed that a new kind of nature preserve be established on some disturbed lands now colonized by rapidly spreading plants, to enable us better to understand the ecological processes at work in landscapes so profoundly affected by human presence.

The success of plant invaders such as amur honeysuckle in a wide range of habitats has prompted scientists to research which traits make these species such formidable competitors. So far there are no certain answers. Still, recent work points to several factors that can help us predict which species are likely to become problems. Probably the best single predictor is whether or not a plant has become invasive somewhere else. If a plant native to, say, Italy has proved invasive in Australia, then introducing it to California, South Africa, or other so-called Mediterranean climates will be risky.

Other important factors have to do with a particular plant's sexual prowess. Many invasive species produce copious amounts of viable seed—those beautiful berries that make us gardeners swoon—and begin reproducing within their first few years. Their seeds tend to have no special germination requirements, such as a period of exposure to cold, and therefore can germinate rapidly. It's not that difficult to screen plants for such traits, a process that could help us predict which proposed introductions have a high potential of spreading rapidly across the landscape.

Reasonable people can disagree about the need for plant regulation. I happen to agree with Neil Diboll that if screening can prevent another purple loosestrife, it is worth a try. Given our current lack of knowledge about the long-term ecological effects of plant invasion, it makes sense for us to strive to prevent future invasions of our few remaining wildlands as we study the dynamics of sites that are already disturbed.

Nevertheless, I came away from the native-plants debate with a good deal of respect for Joachim Wolschke-Bulmahn's perspective as a German landscape historian. He convinced me that, especially at a time of rising anti-immigrant sentiment, we need to be aware that our ideas about nature can have unintended social consequences.

And so we should watch our language, as my mother used to tell me (and sometimes still does). I suggest that we avoid the pervasive terms "alien plant" and "invasive alien." My *Webster's* defines *alien* as follows: "belonging or relating to another person or place—*strange;* relating, belonging or owing allegiance to another country, land or government—foreign; *different in nature or character.*" When we use these terms, we not only risk fanning the flames of xenophobia but also miss the point. The real issue is not place of origin but rather behavior—that is, the problems that invasives cause other plants and animals.

INVASIVE ISN'T THE only dirty word in contemporary horticulture. Another one is *clone.* During the recent brouhaha over the birth of the lamb Dolly, the first mammal ever cloned from a single adult cell, not one politician, ethicist, reporter, or pundit noted that in horticulture cloning has been a routine procedure for decades. In fact, most of the plants found at nurseries today are named cultivars, which are propagated asexually, generally from cuttings (as opposed to sexually, from seed), as that's the only way to preserve choice characteristics of the parent plants, whether a weeping growth habit, giant flowers, or an unusual leaf color. So when you buy, say, *Aster novae-angliae* 'Purple Dome', a New England aster known for its compact, mounded habit as well as its vibrant purple flowers, you're buying a clone—a plant that is genetically identical to every other specimen of 'Purple Dome' in existence. (Clones are those plants that have additional names in single quotes after their two-part botanical names.)

One reason cloning of mammals came later than that of plants is because there are more biological roadblocks to the former. Chop off a human thumb, for example, and you're left with nothing more than a stump, but cut off a shoot of a plant, and it can form adventitious roots; cut off some roots, and they can generate a new shoot system. Leaves can regenerate *both* roots and shoots. Nevertheless, the implications of plant cloning, though less obvious than those of cloning mammals, especially humans, are still worth pondering.

At first glance, asexual propagation would seem to be, as critics claim, an unmitigated disaster for genetic diversity, the most basic level of the diversity of life. But it's not quite so simple. Perhaps we humans are prone to such oversimplifications because we're large animals, and large animals tend to be rather drab in the bedroom department. Whether *Homo sapiens* or giant tortoise, we come in two genders: male and female. We must pair up to reproduce. Period.

But plants! Plants display a (to us) staggering assortment of sexual techniques. For decades, scientists—and scientific journalists—intent on observing evolutionary oddities on far-flung oceanic islands have helped publicize Charles Darwin's voyage in the Galapagos. However, Darwin actually spent most of his time exploring the sexual relations of plants at his home in the Kentish village of Downe. Darwin, and Linnaeus before him, were fascinated by the sex lives of plants. And for good reason, I think. Some plants, such as hollies, are dioecious, meaning that like large animals, each plant is either male or female. Ho-hum. Other plants (the common cane begonia, for instance) are monoecious—that is, individual specimens have separate male

English holly (Ilex aquifolium), *showing branches from a female plant in fruit and in flower, top and bottom left, and part of a branch from a male plant in flower, bottom right.*

and female flowers. Still other plants are hermaphroditic, which is to say that their flowers have both male and female organs. Peer into a corn poppy and beyond the four, typically red petals you'll see a tiny green urn, the female organ called the pistil, surrounded (it figures) by scores of male organs called stamens—long, slender, sticklike filaments topped by pollen-bearing anthers shaped like little coffee beans.

And that's not the least of it. Darwin devoted an entire book, *The Different Forms of Flowers on Plants of the Same Species* (1877), to the distinctions between what he called two "interesting" subgroups of hermaphroditic plants: heterostyled and cleistogamic. Interesting indeed. I like to look at heterostyly as a kind of coquettishness in plants. Some species produce styles (structures attached to the ovary) of two or more lengths to prevent them from being the same height as the male parts, the anthers. This serves to discourage self-fertilization and promote pollination by other flowers from different plants—or, to put it another way, to keep the neighborhood boys at bay and give some handsome strangers a chance. Of course, some plants couldn't care less about handsome strangers; these are the cleistogamous, or self-copulating, plants. Their flowers don't even bother to open, but rather pollinate themselves. Some violet flowers, for example, are cleistogamous. In fact, many plants are capable of "selfing" to one degree or another—that is, fertilizing the female part of the flower with pollen from the same flower. What's more, plant species can reproduce sexually, or asexually, or both.

Who needs to go to the Galapagos when all this is going on in the backyard?

Evolutionary biologists believe that sexual reproduction provides the genetic variation that enables a population to adapt to changing conditions. However, for a population that is already well adapted, asexual reproduction can have its advantages; in effect, it's Mother Nature's version of the adage "If it ain't broke, don't fix it." Grasses reproduce asexually by producing new shoots from their crowns. Eventually, the connection between the offshoot and the parent disintegrates, and a new grass plant—a clone—is established. In some plants, seeds regularly develop from egg cells unfertilized by pollen, in a process called apomixis, representing the ultimate form of single parenting: not even a sperm donor is necessary. The resulting plants are clones as well. Many other kinds of cloning can also be seen in the plant world, including the formation of "daughter" bulbs and corms, the rooting of arching stems that touch the ground, and the growth in euphorbias and other succulents of tiny plantlets along the edges of leaves.

Many horticultural clones have gone on to become important food plants. The 'Bartlett' pear clone originated from a seedling in England around 1770, and the 'Delicious' apple clone was born about a hundred years later as a chance seedling in Jesse Hiatt's orchard in Peru, Iowa. Mealtime as we know it would be very different without clones, but clones have been equally common in ornamental horticulture. They guarantee that we will get the compact New England aster instead of a tall, spindly one for a particular spot in a perennial border, or a highly fragrant, yellow-flowering form of Carolina allspice (*Calycanthus floridus* 'Athens') instead of the species proper with its reddish-brown blooms.

A few cultivars for the flower border or vegetable patch are a good thing. Even in the natural garden, clones have a place: wouldn't it be wonderful, for example, if someone could find a cultivar of native flowering dogwood that would not be susceptible to the anthracnose fungus that has been decimating wild populations? Then, too, it's a safe bet that named cultivars of native trilliums, orchids, and other species threatened by unscrupulous collectors have been propagated vegetatively, not dug up from the wild. So why *not* use them? Nature employs cloning in certain instances—why shouldn't we?

The real problem with cloning is that it's vastly overdone. As a rule, open-pollinated vegetables and ornamentals propagated from seed are a wiser choice. The overuse of clones in agriculture and horticulture is risky because if a major food crop, say, is based on only one or two cultivars, a disease or insect attack can wipe it out. A clone can perpetuate itself successfully in nature, sometimes even better than a plant resulting from a sexual union, but only so long as the environment remains reasonably constant. If the environment changes drastically, a clonally reproduced or highly selfing species may be at a disadvantage because it's less likely to be able to evolve forms better adapted to the new conditions. And in the twenty-first century, change, whether global warming or a spate of new imported insect pests, is undoubtedly in store.

WRITERS DON'T LIKE to admit it, but we often get some of our most important work done in a slightly tipsy state at cocktail parties. That's where I ran into George Robinson, a soft-spoken, bespectacled, and bearded professor of ecology at the State University of New York at Albany. George helped me put in perspective still another reputed threat to life on Earth as we know it: the fragmentation of wild habitat by the haphazard nature of human development. For weeks I'd been daunted by stacks of scientific tomes that I was convinced could shed some light on how our gardens, by dint of their sheer numbers alone, affect biological diversity. One was a collection of U.S. Census Bureau statistics, indicating among other facts that the nation's suburbs have almost doubled in area over the past two decades, and that they consume an additional four hundred square miles every year. You don't have to be a rocket scientist to figure out that as suburbia encroaches on natural areas, there's less room for plants and animals.

During the 1960s, two young biologists named Robert MacArthur and Edward O. Wilson, in a book titled *The Theory of Island Biogeography*, first posited that smaller areas also hold fewer *kinds* of plants and animals. A generation of ecologists influenced by their work has been trying to discover why extinction rates have always been higher on islands than on mainlands, and what this may mean for entire continents whose native communities of plants and animals are currently being carved into bits.

George Robinson is one of these ecologists. As guests wandered around the New York State Museum contemplating a newly unveiled exhibit of natural-history illustrations—everything from exquisite watercolor primulas to precise renderings of reptilian genitalia—George sipped beer, I gulped down a glass of red wine, and we discussed the arcana of applying the theory of island biogeography to suburbia. The study of a century of development on Staten Island undertaken by George and fellow ecologists Stephen Handel and Mary Yurlina seems to support the most basic tenet of island biogeography, that there is a predictable relationship between the size of an island and the number of species it harbors. MacArthur and Wilson calculated that species richness (the technical term for the number of species) doubles with a tenfold increase in area, and, conversely, that a tenfold *decrease* in area may be expected to slash species diversity in half. Unlike the islands they studied, however, Staten Island is not in the middle of an ocean, thousands of miles from the nearest continental landmass; in spots, it's a puny stone's throw from New Jersey. Although George Robinson and his colleagues presented no specific figures on the percentage of land affected by a century's development on Staten Island, they did find that over the past hundred years, as the human population increased tenfold, the number of native plant species was almost halved.

Okay, bigger is unquestionably better as far as healthy natural communities are concerned, but a growing number of biologists believe that no less insidious than the loss of native habitat is the isolation of the remaining fragments. To put this in more familiar horticultural terms, as garden acreage increases, natural areas are getting not only smaller, but also more isolated from each other.

In *The Song of the Dodo*, author David Quammen uses the following metaphor: slice up a fine Persian carpet into a few dozen neat rectangular pieces, and the swatches may together occupy the same area as they did before. But your carpet no longer exists. You're left with a pile of worthless tatters and scraps—just like the scraps of natural landscape that are left when once-unbroken expanses of forest and grassland are sliced up into farms, factories, malls, roads, and gardens. Quammen's argument echoes the prevailing view in conservation biology that habitat fragmentation will disrupt the normal functioning of natural communities and lead sooner or later to species loss.

Well, maybe. As George Robinson patiently pointed out, there's no reason to assume that the high extinction rates found on remote islands will sooner or later become a fact of life on islands of habitat hemmed in by human-dominated land. There are certainly exceptions, but as a rule, most plant seeds and pollinators can much more easily find their way across a local industrial park than across thousands of miles of oceanic wilderness. In another study, "Habitat Fragmentation, Species Diversity, Extinction, and Design of Nature Reserves," Robinson and James Quinn provide impressive evidence suggesting that though total area is important, it's "naive" to conclude that one chunk of land will automatically and always harbor more species than the same area of land cut up into several pieces. In one of their own experiments, they divided a California grassland into a series of fenced plots: two plots each of thirty-two square meters, eight plots of eight square meters, and thirty-two plots of two square meters, for a total of sixty-four square meters in each different "treatment." For four years they followed the turnover of plants in each of these habitat patches, and ultimately found that extinction rates were no higher in the more fragmented sections. This doesn't prove that fragmentation will not take a toll on wild creatures; it just demonstrates that there's no universal formula for calculating its effects. Because it is likely to be harder on some species than on others, Robinson urges that "connectivity" be considered when decisions are made about where to develop the landscape, in an effort to keep damage to a minimum.

Connectivity is something that suburbia apparently lacks. In their Staten Island study, Robinson et al. found that surburbanization was less tolerable for plants and animals than agriculture. During the past hundred years on Staten Island, it has been primarily farmland—not forest or other natural habitat—that's been converted to suburban housing and urban development. The scientists surmised that an agricultural landscape, though vastly different from pristine natural habitat, nonetheless provides opportunities for native species to persist—in woodlots, undrained wetlands, and stream-side corridors as well as hedgerows and other seminatural areas. These areas can play a critical role by, for example, harboring essential pollinators and seed dispersers.

By deliberately designing connectivity into our landscapes, we may be able to avoid another potential pitfall of habitat fragmentation: the splintering of previously continuous "metapopulations" of many species into more or less isolated subpopulations, many of them so small that they carry a substantial risk of extirpation. Small populations are more vulnerable than large ones to a variety of adverse genetic effects. Small populations mean small gene pools; if something goes wrong, it can be big trouble. A new insect pest arrives? A disease takes hold? The climate changes? Small populations can lack the genetic variation needed to cope. Chance—or what scientists call random genetic drift—can take over, and beneficial traits may be lost in the random recombination of genes that occurs during sexual reproduction. In plant species that don't typically grow in small, far-flung populations, so-called inbreeding depression, or interbreeding between closely related individuals, can reduce genetic variation even further, causing such plants to slide still more rapidly toward extinction.

In fragmented landscapes, *out*breeding depression may be no less of a problem, as breeding between different gene pools from different areas can result in individuals that are less likely to survive in *either* area. Gardeners in California, for example, have inadvertently altered the genome of Monterey pine, *Pinus radiata*, a popular ornamental. Because the origin of most plants used for landscaping is unknown, interbreeding of native and planted (and usually not local) trees can easily occur, sometimes causing permanent genetic changes. Scientists have documented such changes in two of the five populations of Monterey pine native to California. In a rapidly urbanizing world that is ever more prone to outbreeding depression and other genetic ills, we gardeners will have to pay greater heed than we do now to the origin, or provenance, of the plants we bring into our landscapes.

If we are to be conscientious gardeners, we need to know a lot more about plant ecology and genetics, processes that are just beginning to be understood by scientists. The commonest measures of genetic diversity, for instance, are based on a small sample of loci, or sites on chromosomes occupied by specific genes—usually fewer than a hundred out of the tens of thousands believed to be of significance in higher organisms. Researchers don't yet know which loci help species to adapt and evolve, and therefore which genetic variations are important to preserve in the face of increasing pressures to choose which populations to save and which to destroy.

We *do* know that the loss or introduction of even a single species can have far-reaching implications for an entire ecosystem—yet another reason for the furor over invasive plants. An ecosystem by definition is a collection of living organisms and their physical environment, all interacting with each other. This complex web of relationships is responsible not only for

Monterey pine (Pinus radiata).

much of the maintenance of biodiversity, but also for the continual generation of new species via evolution. And so the changes we are wreaking on the natural world may mean even less biodiversity over the long haul.

The myriad controversies in contemporary horticulture boil down to one of the most important questions in ecology—in fact, one of the most important questions facing humanity: how much biodiversity is necessary? Does it really make any difference to an ecosystem whether there are many species or few? How many of the millions of species now living on Earth are required to keep natural systems functioning in such a way that they can continue to provide us with what scientists blandly label "ecosystem services"—that is, breathable air, drinkable water, soil healthy enough to yield food, and much more? Would a "weedy" world dominated by the likes of purple loosestrife, from which most species diversity had been lost, remain hospitable to human beings? The honest answer is, *We don't know.*

The uncertainties of the relationship between the diversity of species and a functional biosphere led biologist Paul Ehrlich to formulate the "rivet hypothesis" in 1981. It suggests, in a nutshell, that given the complexity of ecosystems and our lack of detailed knowledge about the way they work, especially in the long run, it's foolish to remove species willy-nilly, just as it would be foolish to pop rivets from an airplane's wing. There are more rivets in an airplane's wing than are strictly necessary to hold it together, but at some point the removal of one more rivet will cause others to pop out, the wing to fail, and the plane to crash. According to the latest evidence, the ability of natural systems to rebound from changing environmental conditions depends on species redundancy—the extra "rivets" that keep the system from flying apart. One reason species diversity is important is that it acts as an insurance policy to cushion the shocks to an ecosystem, whether they're caused by humans or by other forces.

The Staten Island study suggests that even if outright extinctions don't occur immediately, fragmentation tends to shift species' relative abundance within ecosystems, such that the populations of weedy species will increase. At this point it's impossible to say whether the rise of these and the concomitant loss of other species will impair the Earth's ability to sustain us. At the moment, iceplant, *Carpobrotus edulis,* which blankets hundreds of thousands of acres along the southern California coast, is probably holding soils in place as well as did the species-rich mixes of native plants it has replaced. But the ability of such a monoculture to maintain an "ecosystem service" such as erosion control may become more problematic in the longer term, as it may be more vulnerable to a catastrophic disease or less resilient in the face of climate change than the original variety of species.

On the basis of current scientific knowledge, it seems folly to assume that a biologically impoverished world will support us as effectively, or for as long, as one rich in organisms. And even if ecologists someday demonstrate that weedy species are all we need, they won't be able to counter the ethical and aesthetic arguments for preserving the planet's wonderful variety of life forms. These are outside the realm of science, and yet they are some of the most powerful reasons for saving our only known living companions in the universe.

Garden Angst

I CONFESS: FOR years I tried and discarded various garden styles in search of some version of Horticultural Truth. When I moved into my Brooklyn co-op ten autumns ago, the postage-stamp garden wedged between parallel rows of century-old brownstones was everything a garden shouldn't be. Under the towering canopy of hemlock, oak, crabapple, and wild cherry growing in neighboring yards was a scruffy, light-starved patch of lawn. Around the perimeter of the property, enclosed by an imposing stockade fence, an azalea, a yew, and a few wild petunias also struggled to survive, while the irrepressible tree-of-heaven, exemplar of a species that manages to take root in sidewalk cracks and rubble even in the most blighted urban neighborhoods, had a foothold in two corners of the garden.

That winter I set to work, striving, like centuries' worth of gardeners before me, to take control of this unruly horticultural assemblage. I ripped out the tree-of-heaven, turned under the lawn, and double-dug—much to the chagrin of my husband,

Don, who swears that when I'm in one of my gardening frenzies, I appreciate him only for the manly élan with which he lugs around forty-pound bags of "compost and cow poop."

This was my "Sissinghurst phase." Having just returned from Vita Sackville-West's spectacular garden at Sissinghurst, in England (a pilgrimage made by thousands of other American gardeners in recent years), I was determined to create a cottage garden full of plants tumbling over themselves in riotous but harmonious profusion. And like one heavenly corner of Sissinghurst, my cottage garden would be a white garden, with luminous flowers and silvery foliage to attract moths that would hover in the smoggy urban moonlight. I coveted the lacy white festoons of *Rosa longicuspis* draped over the arbor at the center of that glorious garden. I lusted after the drifts of *Lilium regale* poking up through silvery gray artemisia. I would have died for the clouds of *Gypsophila* pierced with the pencils of white *Veronicastrum virginicum* 'Album'.

The images of Sissinghurst dancing in my head aggravated my advanced case of a typical gardener affliction: shade denial. I planted exquisite tree peonies with ruffled white crepe-paper petals, airy clumps of white queen-of-the-prairie, drifts of stately white Madonna lily. One sodden growing season later, most of these sun-loving beauties had succumbed to rot. In subsequent years, like some horticultural equivalent of a shopaholic clotheshorse who empties out his or her closet every year to make room for the latest styles, I went through other phases—my "old-fashioned flowers" phase, for example, when I planted bleeding-heart, foxglove, yellow fumitory, and other antique (and shade-tolerant) flowers that the family of flour merchants who built our brownstone a century before might have cherished. But the nostalgia bug proved as fleeting as the rest of my horticultural fads. Finally, I resolved to think through my aesthetic crisis.

I found a support group in the stacks of the Brooklyn Botanic

Rosa longicuspis
in the white garden at Sissinghurst.

Garden's library. There, in a dusty compendium of essays that grew out of a 1988 symposium at New York's Museum of Modern Art (MOMA), was a bunch of eminent historians, scholars, architects, and landscape designers in an even worse funk than I. The premise of the symposium was that the aesthetics of the twentieth century have been fundamentally hostile to nature; that the modern movement, on the whole, led to a nasty divorce between architecture and nature; that in this century the garden, which traditionally had mediated between human culture and the rest of nature, has become irrelevant; and that the demise of the conventional garden and the absence to date of any vital new gardening tradition represent two of the more troubling aspects of contemporary culture.

I perked up right away.

It seems that the experts have been ringing their hands for decades about the state of modern gardening. In 1937, at the Premier Congrès International des Architectes de Jardins, Achille Duchene proclaimed, "The art of the garden is dead." In an influential three-part series that appeared in *Architectural Record* at around the same time, the modernist landscape architects Garrett Eckbo, Dan Kiley, and James Rose said pretty much the same thing. One of the organizers of the MOMA symposium, William Howard Adams, went on to write a book called *Nature Perfected*, in the last chapter of which, after several hundred pages devoted to the dazzling history of garden design since the days of ancient Egypt, Greece, and Rome, he concludes, "The garden as a work of art, an aesthetic composition beyond the pursuit of horticulture, therapy, or extravagance . . . has all but disappeared from the modern world." Adams then goes on to lament that the "basic elements of composition available to the modern garden-maker have scarcely changed . . . yet they do not seem to be able to produce the poetry and music they once did."

Since as far back as ancient Greece, the major developments in Western landscape design have reflected the scientific and intellectual discoveries of their day. Plato, the mystic and mathematician who lived about four centuries before Christ and was to have a profound influence on Western thought (and garden design) for well over a millennium, taught that there are universal ideas or truths that never change, that have an existence beyond the visible world of matter, man, and time. According to Plato, the human mind is always striving toward this perfection, and the only way to get there is through the constant and eternal principles of mathematics. We can thank Plato for centuries of formal gardens exhibiting geometric precision and perfect symmetry.

Ancient Rome also had a significant effect on Western notions of garden design. A powerful, materialistic society, Rome engendered an appreciation of the beauty of landscape and an idealization of country life in the poetry of Virgil, Ovid, and Horace (an appreciation that survives to this day in such blockbuster publications as Hearst's *Country Living* magazine). With the emergence of wealthy and well-traveled landowners, the cult of the country house was born. In the first century after Christ, the younger Pliny left detailed descriptions of what the perfect villa should look like. The architecture was to be formal, with views of the sea or countryside and cool porticoes with romantic wall paintings that integrated the house with the garden. The garden was to be formal, too, with shady promenades, clipped hedges, box parterres, topiary, and sculpture collected from the far-flung corners of the empire.

The secluded, geometric gardens of the Middle Ages, walled off from the fallen earthly world, were modeled after the Garden of Eden and the *hortus conclusus*, or enclosed garden, of the Canticles. During the Italian Renaissance, which looked back to Greece and Rome rather than to the church for authority, humans truly became the measure of all things. Lorenzo di Medici and his circle saw themselves as the heirs of Plato and strove to re-create the cultured life they read about in Horace

An Italian Renaissance garden.

and Pliny. The garden became a setting for pleasure and philosophical debate.

Gardens of the Italian Renaissance were strictly geometrical, displaying a self-conscious human control over the landscape in their axial layouts. The strict mathematical precision of the garden was echoed in the architecture of Palladio, who carried the theory of Platonic geometry to its ultimate form. This classical conception of space represented a search, through geometry, for a divine harmony between man and the universe, of which man considered himself to be the center. Not only the form but also the elements of the Italian Renaissance garden—evergreens, stone, and water—were Platonic. Here again, box parterres, clipped hedges, stands of dark cypress and groves of holly, sculpture, stairways, and water in repose and in fountains expressed permanence rather than ephemerality.

From the predictable, ordered world of Renaissance ratio and proportion, the West plunged into the Baroque period, an age of tension, fear, and metaphysical uncertainty. (Now, *this* was a time we can relate to!) It was an era of immense scientific ferment, as astronomical discoveries, combined with the questioning of religious dogma, knocked existing beliefs for a loop.

Early in the sixteenth century, Copernicus offered statistical evidence for the hypothesis that the Earth was not a fixed point in space, but rather one of several planets that both turned on their axes and revolved around the sun. Galileo produced a body of work that supported this theory, for which he was promptly excommunicated by the church. In 1609, Kepler proved that the planets moved around the sun in elliptical orbits, destroying another cherished assumption, which held that all heavenly bodies moved in perfect circles. It was beginning to look as if we humans were simply a part of some swirling, infinite complex far beyond our understanding.

Baroque landscapes reflected these dizzying developments.

The landscape surrounding the Villa Orsini in Bomarzo, for example, was peopled by primitive giants, seemingly bent upon the destruction of puny humans. Architectural structures were tilted, askew. The grotto of the Pitti Palace in Florence, designed by Buontalenti around 1590, is downright hallucinogenic, depicting a grotesque world where nothing seems secure: the paintings inside have no consistent perspective, and rocks grow into men or beasts.

In the seventeenth century, the French monarchy got a grip on things, and law and order returned to the garden. In the landscapes of André Le Nôtre, particularly Versailles, the growing fascination with the laws of optics and perspective was used to full effect, the eye being directed firmly, with no freedom to roam, from the palace down axial and radial avenues. The avenues themselves were lined with trees and punctuated by sculpture seen against clipped *charmilles*, or hedges. Within these heroic compositions fit for the gods were intricate parterres, canals, fountains, triumphal arches, and treillages. The seventeenth-century French garden expressed total conquest over time, space, and organic nature. Absolute geometric form was imposed on the landscape down to the smallest detail, with nary an errant blade of grass. Throughout Europe, this kind of autocratic garden became de rigueur for anyone wealthy enough to own a country villa or palace.

In the eighteenth century, absolute monarchy began to seem increasingly distasteful, particularly in Holland and England, and with it its supreme expression in landscape design. In his *Essay Concerning Human Understanding*, published in 1690, John Locke, one of the founders of the empiricist school of philosophy, argued against any "innate ideas" and insisted that humans instead derived all ideas from experience—thereby contradicting the divine right of kings. In the *Spectator* papers on the "Pleasures of the Imagination," Joseph Addison emphasized the new importance of nature in the origin of ideas. When we explore the "wide fields of Nature," he wrote, our eyes "wander up and down without confinement," and our minds are "fed with an infinite variety of Images." These simple visual pictures in turn awaken "numberless ideas that before slept in the Imagination." A natural, irregular, asymmetrical garden suited the intellectual atmosphere of the Enlightenment much better than the old Platonic gardens of geometry.

Once again, ancient Greece and Rome proved handy models. The rise of the English landscape garden at the turn of the century was part of the quest to establish England as the new Athens. The nation was now ruled by Parliament, and Parliament was in turn controlled by the landed gentry, whose primary interest lay in the quality of life on its members' country estates. Not surprisingly, the English squirearchy sang the praises of the country life first celebrated by ancient Roman poets.

Beginning in the mid–fifteenth century and continuing well into the seventeenth, much of England's acreage was transformed from a land of vast forests and heaths to enclosed, cultivated farmland owned by the nobility. This gradual taming of the countryside provided yet another impetus for the eighteenth-century English landscape garden. Technology had an impact on the craft of gardening, too. As long as gardens were enclosed, their relationship with the larger landscape—that is, with nature—was inevitably limited. The ha-ha, a sunken barrier shaped like a dry moat, obviated the need for fencing to keep animals out of the garden and therefore made possible an uninterrupted view out into the countryside. With his invention of the ha-ha, landscape designer William Kent, in the words of Horace Walpole, "leapt the fence and saw all nature was a garden." A new knowledge of foreign cultures, especially Chinese gardens with their sinuous curves, also influenced the development of landscape design. Sound familiar? The same three forces—the human domination of the landscape, the rise of technology, and the globalization of culture—have intensified over the past three hundred years and continue to shape landscape design today.

The typical English landscape garden consisted of undulating expanses of grass leading down to an irregularly shaped body of water over which a bridge arched; trees were grouped casually, and classically inspired houses and other buildings could be glimpsed in the distance. At first, the new English gardens owed a lot to the landscape paintings of Claude Lorrain and Nicolas Poussin, with their re-creation of classical legends. For example, the gardens of Stourhead, begun around 1740, were studded with temples and other allusions that made up a classical allegory in landscape of man's passage through the world. A closed walk around an artificial lake began with birth at the Temple of Flora, wound around to the grottoes of the Underworld, emerged at the Pantheon of earthly glories, and passed through a rock arch representing mortality before ascending heavenward at the Temple of Apollo.

For at least half a century, the English garden sublimated the conflict between rationalism and empiricism, the two rival philosophies of the Western world. George Plumptre, in his book *The Garden Makers*, poignantly notes that the gardens of the first few decades of the eighteenth century embodied a wonderful quality that resulted "when the pendulum reached the midpoint between rationalism and empiricism, between geometrical symmetry and regularity and asymmetry and the use of serpentine curves." The reaction against "unnatural" formality eventually led, in the second half of the century, to the work of Capability Brown, who largely ditched the buildings and other classical allusions in favor of rolling land, water, and clumps of trees in his landscapes.

At the time, philosophers George Berkeley and David Hume were taking the work of Locke to its logical conclusion. The empiricists rejected the claims of Plato and his followers that there were magnificent realms of perfect knowledge that could

An eighteenth-century English landscape garden.

be perceived by human reason; like Locke, they maintained that all knowledge came from sense experience. Hume concluded that because our only source of information is the impressions we gain from our senses, a great deal of what we *think* we know is actually an illusion. What we perceive via our senses is qualities such as colors, sounds, and shapes—qualities that don't necessarily belong to "material" or "external" objects. It's only our curious psychological makeup that informs our view of the world around us. Another way of putting this is that there is a fundamental division between the separate and independent realms of mind and matter.

The empiricists laid the philosophical foundation for science. The age-old quest for absolute knowledge came to be seen as fruitless; scientists aimed not to prove any metaphysical truths but only to develop probable hypotheses about the world and how it worked. They conceived of the Earth as a giant machine whose parts could be analyzed one at a time through rigorous and objective application of what came to be known as the scientific method. The knowledge thus gained could be applied through technology to gain power over nature.

By the nineteenth century, science and technology had indeed radically expanded our ability to control our physical environment. All this technical ingenuity left its mark on garden design as well. Coal furnaces heated greenhouses and the brick walls of kitchen gardens, while steam engines were harnessed to throw fountain jets far into the air. Hothouses and greenhouses became frequent features of the Victorian garden, as the new species being brought back from the far ends of the Earth by plant explorers, particularly tender flowers from the tropics, had to be accommodated. By the 1840s, an elaborate bedding system had evolved, completely replacing the eighteenth-century desire to replicate nature.

By 1850, as many Britons lived in urban as in rural areas, and the earlier notion of a civic landscape emanating from country life had pretty much petered out. By the end of the century, the population had tripled, roads crisscrossed the countryside, cities were spilling into suburbs, and huge tracts had been ravaged by industrialism.

It was against this backdrop that William Robinson railed against the "Dark Ages of flower gardening" and led the revolt against the importation of exotic plants and their use in the "pastry-cook style" of carpet bedding. In *The English Flower Garden* and other works, he advocated a more informal landscape employing native and suitable nonindigenous perennials rather than the ranks of greenhouse-raised annuals from tropical and subtropical climes around the globe. The herbaceous border, which reached its epitome as landscape art in the work of painter-turned-plantswoman Gertrude Jekyll, was a variation on this theme of floral informality, as is the interest in wildflower meadows and old-fashioned cottage garden flowers in the United States today.

DURING MY SOJOURN in the library, it dawned on me that contemporary gardening philosophy is out of whack with the theories evolving on the frontiers of science and advanced thought. One of the strongest impulses in American gardening today stems from the old hippie urge to "go back to the land"— to leave the rat race in the city for the "simple life" on farms or in the woods, where you can grow all your own food organically. The gurus of this movement were Ken and Barbara Kern and Helen and Scott Nearing, who in the 1970s published treatises for city slickers like me on everything from how to graft a scion onto a rootstock to how to milk a cow without getting kicked. I cut my teeth on this kind of gardening, and I'm still hooked— every time one of those confounded car alarms goes off, I reach instinctively for a back-to-the-land bible such as the Kerns' *Owner-Built Homestead*. These days, alas, even back-to-the-land gardening has gotten complicated. It's no longer good enough to grow a pesticide-free tomato; you have to be the first on your rural route (or, in my case, urban block) to have the latest rediscovered-heirloom, open-pollinated, yellow-fleshed variety.

As I began to fancy myself a more sophisticated gardener, I gravitated more toward the other major impulse in modern American horticulture: the cult of the herbaceous border. Try as we may to Americanize the flower border by throwing in a few shrubs or indigenous perennials, it remains a turn-of-the-century impressionist painter's vision of landscape for the English upper class—which, of course, is a big part of the reason we anglophiles love it.

Both the rustic, back-to-the-land American and the painterly, aristocratic English approaches to contemporary gardening are, however, rooted in visions of nature that no longer ring true. The poet and philosopher Frederick Turner has distinguished between gardens that imitate what nature *is* and those that imitate what nature *looks like*. You could say that the neo-Platonic practitioners of the "hippie" approach seek that essence or truth in Nature which remains unchanged beyond the shifting masks of mutability and horticultural fashion. By way of contrast, the romantic gardens of those who follow the painterly path, in the tradition of Gertrude Jekyll and Vita Sackville-West, reflect the more recent empiricist philosophy that holds that we humans can never know what is the form or essence of something; all we can know is colors, shapes, and other sensations.

The twentieth century has brought more than its share of devastating blows to prevailing beliefs, beginning in 1907 with Albert Einstein's theory of relativity, which obliterated the concept of absolute time and space. Meanwhile, the human population approaches six billion. Space flight has revealed vast areas of tropical jungle, which once seemed the last refuge from human domination, going up in smoke. Cities have expanded far beyond the size that can be supported by their regional environments. Industrialization has begun to alter nature on a global scale, rupturing the Earth's protective ozone layer, disrupting the planet's carbon cycle, and threatening climate change on a massive scale. Thousands, if not millions, of species face imminent extinction.

What is the place of landscape design in such a world? As William Howard Adams points out in *Nature Perfected*, the pressure of massive overpopulation and monstrous cities has raised critical questions about the form, the function, and even the very survival of gardens. "Concocting bogus images of lost paradise," in his view, "only exposes our impoverishment." It seems that we are being forced back to something akin to the "walled gardens of some barbarous medieval town," he writes, "but without any of the metaphysics to transform our isolation into a civilized, revitalizing environment."

Is there any way out of this horticultural—and metaphysical—abyss?

Ever since the Renaissance, our thinking on the subject of nature and culture has swung wildly between the rationalist or classical and the empiricist or romantic, with only a few short-lived reprieves, as in the early-eighteenth-century English landscape garden, wherein the two were temporarily reconciled. For the rationalist, culture is the realm of freedom and perfection; for the romantic, nature is. Both basically assume that human beings are different and separate from nature.

This nature-culture dualism, as it's been called, ignores some of the central tenets of twentieth-century science, including the principal scientific theory of evolution, which holds that we are descended from other animal species. It likewise ignores the most important implication of the quantum theory, which, according to Princeton physicist John Wheeler, destroyed the concept of the world as "sitting out there," outside of and apart from us. The act of observation in itself makes the observer a participator; making a measurement, even of an electron, changes the state of the electron to the degree that the universe will never be quite the same again.

The nature-culture dualism also fails to acknowledge another fundamental idea of twentieth-century science: the ecosystem concept. First articulated by Alfred George Tansley in 1935, this theory suggests that nature functions and is inextricably connected not only at the molecular level, as conventional reductionist thinking has implied, but at *every* level. Just as in the eighteenth century an explosion of knowledge was balanced by a feeling for the romantic landscape, so in twentieth-century society does ecology fulfill a similar function—not only because it satisfies an emotional need but also because we know instinctively that a lack of appreciation of nature and our role in it threatens life as we know it.

In *Mind and Nature: A Necessary Unity*, the late anthropologist Gregory Bateson argued that the rise of ecology was essentially an impulse to unify and thereby sanctify the natural world, of which we are a part. All the great religions and epistemologies, he noted, are alike in stressing an ultimate unity. The Western world's loss of the sense of aesthetic unity experienced during the Renaissance, he wrote, "was, quite simply, an epistemological mistake." Bateson was concerned above all with the fundamental unities and patterns that underlie the apparent diversity of living things. The mental system that governs how we think and learn, he asserted, is the very same sort of system that governs the evolution and ecology of all life on Earth. He termed this pattern of patterns (or meta-pattern) connecting mind and nature a "stochastic process," defined as a sequence of events that combines a random component with a selective process in such a way that only certain aspects of the random endure. In the case of evolution, this process involves random genetic changes accompanied by natural selection; in the case of the human mind, it involves random processes of trial and error in thought, accompanied by selective reinforcement. Both processes partly interact with and are partly isolated from each other—one within populations, the other within the individual;

one a matter of multiple generations of many individuals, the other a matter of a single lifetime. In each case, both fit together to form a single, ongoing biosphere.

Another theory that describes a meta-pattern connecting the human and natural worlds is the Gaia hypothesis, first posited by independent scientist James Lovelock in the 1970s. It argues that in a sense, the Earth is a giant feedback system, and that all living things, ourselves included, play an active role in maintaining its atmosphere, climate, and chemical environment—indeed, all conditions optimal for life. The Gaia hypothesis is an alternative to the traditional view that nature is a primitive force to be subdued and conquered, and to the equally distressing picture of the planet as forever orbiting, driverless and purposeless, around the sun.

In short, our culture is in the midst of a cosmological transformation. Contemporary science, especially biology and physics, suggests that it is no longer good enough to create gardens that merely look like nature. Twentieth-century science is leading the way to a new perception of the natural world and our place in it. A new kind of garden that can reunify abstract thought and natural form will be its consummate expression.

The modern approach to landscape design in the early decades of this century offered glimmers of such a new garden. Dan Kiley and Jim Rose on the East Coast and Thomas Church in California made it possible to cast off preconceived notions of design and to develop gardens based on the character of specific sites and on the user's needs. The even more radical concept of organic form was put into practice in landscape design by Jens Jensen and in architecture by Frank Lloyd Wright. In Jensen's prairie landscapes nature, not style, determined form; indeed, nature *was* style.

My hunch is that the next great age of ecological garden design will build on this notion of organic form. The ecological garden won't try to imitate, like classical gardens, what nature is, or, like romantic gardens, what it looks like. As Frederick Turner has suggested, the new garden instead must *act* like nature, must do what nature does. And what nature does is reproduce itself, copy itself into the future, gradually improving on the copies by means of the evolutionary forces of sexual reproduction, mutation, and selection. Biology, particularly ecology and genetics, is transforming landscape design into a super-art whose palette will include ecological interdependence and species evolution.

To create the new garden, we need to know a great deal more about how ecologies function. Another glimmer of the future landscape can be seen in the work of those scientists who over the past few decades have been learning to restore disturbed ecological communities. Restoration ecologist William R. Jordan III has described this work as a deliberate attempt to compensate for humankind's adverse influences on ancient ecosystems such as the North American tallgrass prairie. If these ancient communities of species are to survive, we, the most complex and far-reaching species of all, must attend to their continuance—in the home garden as well as in the larger landscape.

Gardens That Act like Nature

TO MOST PEOPLE, a landscape is a scene, an idyllic picture—
an abstract, almost static form. Ever since it first came into the
English language in the early seventeenth century, the noun
landscape has been bound up in painterly notions of place.
According to the *Oxford English Dictionary*, when English-
speakers first uttered the word, sometime around 1603—just four
years before the establishment of the first permanent English
colony in Virginia—what they meant was a "picture representing
natural inland scenery."

By the following century, William Kent and other founders
of the English landscape garden were unabashedly grafting contemporary French and Italian painters' conceptions of the classical landscape onto the English countryside. Kent, called the
"father of modern gardening" by Horace Walpole, was himself a
painter who set about remaking the English landscape after
returning from an extended stay in Rome, where he studied
art. This pictorial idea of space, imported by wealthy colonists,

took firm root in American soil. American gardens today are still shaped by such eighteenth-century notions of landscape, as well as by those of yet another English painter, Gertrude Jekyll, for whom land was a canvas and plants the medium with which to explore color. This painterly approach is a carryover, perhaps, from the days when we could perceive only the beauty of nature's surfaces, not the complex patterns and processes underlying them.

The ecological garden re-creates the inherent elegance of these living processes and celebrates them in visible forms. It's impossible to create a garden that acts like nature without understanding how nature works—and that means boning up on biology, especially ecology.

Uh-oh: if biology is the mother of garden design, then I'm in big trouble. And so, probably, are a lot of other gardeners.

Almost every American goes through the rite of passage known as tenth-grade biology, from the boring lectures on mitosis to the dissection of dead fetal pigs. Is it any wonder that our gardens are so lifeless? I was lucky. My high school biology teacher was a perky, miniskirt-clad, and very pregnant blonde whose lessons on gametes and gestation were rather graphically illustrated by her ever-expanding belly. Still, I held my nose through every science class in my subsequent academic career. Over the past few years, however, I've had to dust off twenty-year-old bits of biology retrieved from atrophied regions of my brain. I've consulted classic tomes such as those by Frederic Clements, one of the trailblazers of early-twentieth-century botany, as well as works by practitioners such as aquatic biologist John Todd, at the very cutting edge of ecological design today. The collective wisdom of those who have spent lifetimes studying the inner workings of ecosystems offers a wealth of ideas for gardeners seeking a more life-affirming approach.

The term "ecosystem" has been around only for about sixty years—a blink of an eye in the evolution of human culture. In

1935, in a twenty-three-page technical paper entitled "The Use and Abuse of Vegetational Concepts and Terms," the English ecologist Alfred George Tansley introduced this new word to the world. Tansley defined an ecosystem as a system comprising not only living organisms but also their physical-chemical environment, all acting together. From the point of view of the ecologist, he wrote, ecosystems "are the basic units of nature on the face of the Earth." There are different kinds of ecosystems, he noted, and they come in various sizes. Tansley considered ecosystems part of the physical hierarchy; in his words, "They form one category of the multitudinous physical systems of the universe, which range from the universe as a whole down to the atom."

Seven years after the publication of Tansley's paper, his new term was applied in one of the classics of modern ecology, a study of Cedar Bog Lake in Minnesota by a young scientist named Raymond Lindeman. Lindeman advanced Tansley's idea in several important ways. He demonstrated that nature is organized into recognizable ecological systems, such as lakes. These ecosystems have a structure, defined as the network of feeding relations among their various species—the network now commonly known as the food chain. The species can be organized into groups: those that make their own food through photosynthesis (i.e., green plants), those that feed directly on living plants (herbivores), those that feed on herbivores (predators), and those that feed on dead organic material (decomposers). The ecosystem processes not only energy from the sun (and occasionally from other sources) but also chemical elements, or nutrients. The energy flows and the nutrients cycle among the various populations of species and between the living organisms and their physical environment.

In recent decades, the biological sciences have been blessed with a handful of practitioners who have been able to bring their work to life for a popular audience. Here, Paul Ehrlich and Edward O. Wilson come immediately to mind, as does Eugene

Odum. The term "ecosystem" remained part of a technical argot until Odum, an ecologist in the Department of Zoology at the University of Georgia, published his *Fundamentals of Ecology* in 1953. Odum made the ecosystem concept a central tenet of his widely used textbook, which examines the data and ideas developed by Lindeman and others. The book has had a huge influence both on a new generation of biologists and on the general public.

Even so, thirty years ago the ecosystem as a scientific concept was still fuzzy, lacking as it was a coherent, or deep, body of knowledge to back it up. This began to change in the late 1960s and early '70s, when staff, funds, and facilities were directed on a massive scale to ecosystem research. Several new paths were blazed by F. Herbert Bormann and Gene E. Likens, who extended ecosystem studies from lakes, with their obvious edges, to terrestrial systems, using the watershed as the identifiable boundary at their Hubbard Brook, New Hampshire, research site. They also manipulated the ecosystem to discover how it would respond to disturbance and stress.

The ecosystem has become a key element not only of a new scientific discipline but also of a new worldview. In his book on the history of the ecosystem concept, ecologist Frank Benjamin Golley writes that Western science and philosophy have traditionally tended "to decompose every object into its components, then to declare that all important properties reside in these components." The new emphasis on ecosystems, by contrast, encourages us to adopt a holistic view of nature and how it works. This holistic view "is not the 'right' view," says Golley, "it is merely another way of looking at the world." In fact, new technology has given us the tools to consider ever larger wholes, as remote sensing and computer processing of remote-sensed data have enabled us to see clearly the larger systems of which the ecosystem is a part, from the local landscape to the regional biome to the global biosphere.

The ecosystem concept is also key to the future of the gar-den. It is the ultimate model for restructuring the means by which we humans sustain ourselves, without destroying the creatures with which we share the Earth.

Over the past century or so, we've learned that natural systems are defined by two major kinds of order: structural and functional. A terrestrial ecosystem's structure, or form, depends primarily on its vegetation, meaning that the structure of a grass-land is very different from that of a forest, for example, because of the form of the predominant plant life. By the same token, the functions of these two plant communities—that is, how they respond to fire, wind damage, and other types of disturbance, and how they use and recycle water, nutrients, organic matter, and so on—differ because of the differences in their physical environ-ments, including the soils, climate, and other conditions that give rise to them.

In the natural landscape, form is innate; it arises from within, in response to climate, geology, and terrain. But in the traditional Western garden, a predetermined pattern has been imposed on nature.

American architects in the early decades of this century were the first to apply a notion of innate or organic form to the design of human habitat. While the Modernists, led by Le Corbusier, sought to impart form to industrial processes, Frank Lloyd Wright developed a modern architecture that sprang from the soil rather than from the machine. Wright believed that a build-ing should evolve from its site, climate, materials, and function as a human shelter. He wrote that his first Prairie house "began to associate with the ground and become natural to its prairie site," which was vast, flat, horizontal. In Arizona, he saw the intrinsic structure of local plants such as cacti as an analogue for a new kind of desert architecture. The natural environment and the potential user's character and purpose, as well as the struc-ture's intended function, were the germinating force, like the

DNA of a tree, from which the building's ideal form should emerge.

At around the same time, Jens Jensen and other Chicago designers were developing a new landscape art for the prairie region that reflected a keen appreciation of the aesthetic personalities of native plant communities in the grasslands. But Wright and Jensen and their followers had the distinction, as well as the bad luck, of being ahead of their time. Their notion of organic form was just beginning to encompass ecological structure, which was being described by scientists of their day, but it did not embrace ecological function; the ecosystem concept had barely been broached, and so while their creations could allude aesthetically to the patterns of nature, they could not integrate its processes.

During the past few decades, we've begun to understand both the visible patterns and the processes of natural communities. The science of ecology tells us that our gardens are not isolated slivers of land, that what we do with our home landscapes has a ripple effect on larger, natural systems. And the effect of traditional gardening has been substantially negative.

In the garden, as elsewhere, we have replaced nature's continual cycling and recycling of materials with what John Tillman Lyle, professor of landscape architecture at the California State Polytechnic University, calls a system of one-way flows, from source (in the case of fertilizer, mines or natural-gas fields) to consumption (the garden) to sink (the groundwater or receiving waterway where fertilizer runoff ends up). Measured by the values of the marketplace, as Lyle notes in *Regenerative Design for Sustainable Development*, this new industrial-design concept has worked remarkably well: "Success fed its expansion; by the beginning of the last quarter of the twentieth century, the global landscape had been almost entirely reorganized to facilitate the artificial system of one-way flows." By 1988, according to the World Resources Institute, a Washington, D.C.–based environmental think tank, "source" landscapes—agricultural and grazing lands, oil fields, mines, commercial forests, and watersheds—covered about 61 percent of the global land area. But source materials are being taken from the Earth far more quickly than they can be replaced naturally in the wild. In Lyle's words, "Herein lies the modern crisis of resource depletion and degradation. The global statistics on deforestation, desertification, salinization, soil erosion, habitat loss, and other landscape pathologies tell that story very clearly."

While the sources are being depleted, the sinks—the entire atmosphere, most streams, rivers, lakes, bays, and wetlands, and most groundwater and waste dumps—are being overloaded. Hence urban smog, the buildup of carbon dioxide and other global-warming gases in the atmosphere, polluted waterways, overflowing landfills, and toxic contamination of air, land, and water. Eventually, a one-way throughput system destroys the very landscapes on which it depends.

A garden that acts like nature is not designed for one-way flows. It is integrated with natural cycling processes and therefore minimizes environmental destruction. The way to integrate a garden with natural processes is through design—by creating a human ecosystem that reflects, and in some cases even faithfully re-creates, the structure and function of an appropriate natural model.

GOOD GARDENERS ARE by definition quite attentive to the needs of their individual plants. They know that every plant has a certain tolerance range, or a limit as to the extremes of, say, temperature that it can survive: camellias, for instance, flourish in the Carolinas but will perish without winter protection much farther north. More sophisticated gardeners know the natural history of their plants and therefore not only how cold-hardy they are but also what types of soil and exposure they prefer. Black-eyed Susan and threadleaf coreopsis are adapted to the lean, often dry soils characteristic of their native prairie habitats, while foamflowers, native to North American forests, thrive in the moist, rich, organic soils of the woodland floor; the prairie perennials bask in the full sun of their grassland habitats, while the foamflowers grow in the cool, dappled shade of the forest canopy.

This kind of information may serve to keep alive plants that are far removed from their natural ranges, but it offers only the most rudimentary guidance for garden designers. The golden rule of horticulture, which admonishes gardeners to choose the "right plant for the site," merely suggests that in selecting which plants to combine, we would do well to put plants with similar requirements together. In other words, it's not smart to put a drought lover in a bog, but there is a certain logic to pairing it with other plants similarly adapted to dry conditions. Beyond this, we gardeners are on our own, and most of us end up making design decisions based on purely aesthetic considerations such as flower or leaf color. Although the golden rule generally offers a large palette of plants from which to choose, it ignores crucial ecological considerations such as the competition among various species, the productivity or actual number of individual plants that the natural fertility of a soil can support, or the diversity of species that the land will allow—the kinds of considerations that so far have made nature a much better gardener than us, cloaking the planet with a breathtaking diversity of plant and associated animal life.

Ecological garden design requires more than the golden rule. A specialized branch of ecology that focuses on plant communities provides a wealth of ideas about plant selection, plant combination, and plant placement, the three things at the heart of the landscape designer's art.

One of the basic ways scientists determine the structure of ecosystems is by measuring species diversity. This measure is an accounting not only of the total number of species but also of how evenly distributed those species are, or, conversely, the degree to which a particular species dominates the entire community. Consider, for instance, the coastal oak forests of Shelter Island, a sleepy isle sandwiched between the North and South Forks of eastern Long Island, where Don and I spend peaceful summer weekends listening to ospreys and flickers instead of our city neighbor's seemingly inexhaustible collection of Mario Lanza albums. These forests consist of only a few canopy tree species: black oak, white oak, wild cherry, and white and sweet birch. The oaks, especially the black oaks, outnumber the birches by about ten to one, and the cherries dominate the forest edges. Stands of sassafras are broken occasionally by shad or flowering dogwood in the subcanopy tree layer. The number of species in Shelter Island's forests is relatively small, perhaps because the island's poor, sandy soils can't support more biodiversity. By comparison, in the heart of the mixed deciduous forests of the Cumberland Mountains and parts of the Allegheny and Cumberland plateaus, there is no single dominant tree. The forest comprises about three dozen species of trees, among them beech, white basswood, sugar maple, yellow poplar, sweet buckeye, red and white oak, magnolia, birch, white ash, and cherry. These forests represent the height of diversity in the eastern deciduous forests.

In the words of Sim Van der Ryn and Stuart Cowan, an architect and a mathematician, respectively, who collaborated on a book on this subject, "Ecological design, at the deepest level, is design for biodiversity." Biodiversity, they write, is the "most exquisite form of complexity in the world." It is also the true harvest of several billion years' worth of evolutionary design on the part of nature.

There are two good reasons for gardeners to design for diversity. For one, hundreds of species of native plants in the United States alone will not survive the twenty-first century unless we plant and tend them. The same goes for the open-pollinated heirloom food plants that are increasingly being replaced by modern hybrids in the trade, despite the fact that these, too, represent a vast storehouse of genetically diverse and locally adapted crops. Seeding a garden with diversity is also critical for its health and resiliency. There is a threshold of diversity beyond which a farm or food garden will become resistant to pests, diseases, and weeds, or maintain soil fertility by, for example, incorporating a smattering of nitrogen-fixing plants. Without this diversity, gardens and larger-scale agricultural systems must remain dependent upon fertilizers, pesticides, and other inputs.

The characteristic type of vegetation native to a particular area is another key to ecosystem structure. Before Tansley invented the ecosystem concept, the science of ecology was dominated by this aspect of vegetation structure. In the United States, nobody furthered its study more than the indefatigable Frederic Clements. Raised and educated in the state of Nebraska, at a time when the vegetation of the western states had not yet been greatly altered by agriculture, Clements traveled extensively across the continent as a researcher for the Carnegie Institution in Washington, D.C., an important source of support for the then-young science of plant ecology. He was usually chauffeured by his wife, Edith, a trained botanist in her own right who reportedly also pitched in as secretary, photographer, translator, and sometimes coauthor. Based on his experiences and observations, Clements came up with a theory of vegetation that he then fleshed out in a series of volumes published between 1905 and 1939. Tansley called him "by far the greatest individual creator of the modern science of vegetation."

Clements described much of the vegetation of North America, naming regional variations. He pointed out that just as higher plants can be divided into root, stem, leaf, flower, and fruit on the basis of structure and functions, so, too, can vegetation be divided into forest, grassland, chaparral, tundra, and other types, all determined by the regional climate. These he

called plant formations. He also observed that formations themselves consist of various associations—for example, the tallgrass
prairie of the Midwest and the shortgrass prairie of the Great
Plains are both part of the great American grassland formation.
According to Clements, these regional "climax" plant communities are the most diverse and complex possible in their particular
climates and terrains.

As Clements put it, "An airplane view of the continent of
North America would reveal the fact that it is covered by three
great types of vegetation, namely, forest, scrub, and grassland"
(an airplane view in *his* day, perhaps, but not today, when it
would probably reveal mostly lawn). Closer scrutiny, at least
back then, would reveal the myriad formations and associations.
Just south of the polar ice cap is the Arctic tundra, an expanse of
permafrost on which grow mostly low or dwarf shrubs, lichens,
and mosses. Beneath that is a vast area of deep green coniferous
forest of spruce, larch, balsam fir, jack pine, aspen, and birch;
known as the taiga or boreal forest, it stretches across the continent from the Atlantic coastline of central Labrador to the
mountains and interior and central coastal plains of Alaska. As
it dips down into the northern reaches of Minnesota, Michigan,
New York, and New England, its conifers mingle with sugar
maple and other deciduous trees. A related forest flows down the
spine of the Appalachians as far as North Carolina.

Yet another vast coniferous forest dominates the western
third of North America. It includes the lush, moss-draped rain
forests and old-growth forests of Douglas fir and coast redwood in
the Pacific Northwest, the sunny stands of ponderosa pine and
quaking aspen in the Rocky Mountain states, and the groves of
giant sequoia in the Sierra Nevada. These are among the world's
most magnificent forests. In the southern reaches of this formation may be found an association of pygmy conifer woodlands
dominated by low-growing junipers and piñon pines.

The eastern half of the United States, for its part, is dominated by deciduous trees. The eastern deciduous forest formation encompasses many associations, ranging from the oak and chestnut forests of the Middle Atlantic coast (the chestnuts of which have been devastated by blight) to the maple and basswood forests of southern Wisconsin and Minnesota. The color of these deciduous forests changes dramatically with the seasons. A sprightly yellow-green in spring, they mature to a deep green in summer and explode into a fireball of color in autumn before settling into an iridescent winter gray.

South and east of the deciduous forests is a formation called the coastal plain, an area of salt marshes, cypress swamps, and pine forests. It includes much of what is still called the Deep South, but it also extends north and east as far as the pitch-pine barrens of New Jersey, sweeps around the bottom of the Appalachians to the Gulf Coast forests dominated by longleaf and slash pines, and reaches up the Mississippi River valley as far as southern Illinois.

Although northern Florida is deep in the southern pinelands of the coastal plain, on the southern tip of the state is a splash of flora related to the tropical forests of southern Mexico, Central America, and the Caribbean islands. Edging the coast, meanwhile, is a forest of stilt-rooted mangroves. In southern Florida the land flattens out and is cut by broad, shallow rivers thickly populated with saw grass. These immense sedge prairies, or everglades, are occasionally interrupted by raised clumps, or hammocks, of dense tropical forest.

West of the Appalachian Mountains, deciduous forest gives way to open woodland, or savanna, and eventually to prairie. While humid climates support forests and arid climates support deserts, the prairie thrives on a moisture level somewhere in between the two. Unlike deserts, grasslands have a solid ground cover of vegetation; unlike forests, they feature open space and endless vistas. Moving westward in the grassland formation, the tallgrass prairie turns into shortgrass plains as rainfall decreases from thirty to fifteen inches annually.

The shortgrass plains.

West of the prairies is the intermountain region, a vast area of arid western North America sandwiched between the Rocky Mountains and the Sierra Nevada. All four deserts of the United States fall within its boundaries. The Great Basin Desert spreads north from Utah and Nevada; its northernmost reaches comprise the sagebrush steppes of eastern Oregon, southern Idaho, and western Wyoming, an area of austere beauty dominated by sagebrush, saltbush, and grasses. The Mojave Desert straddles the borders where California, Nevada, and. Arizona meet, and extends into the extreme southwestern corner of Utah. Unlike the Great Basin Desert, the Mojave is dotted with cacti and yucca, and annual flowers explode into a short-lived kaleidoscope of color in spring. One yucca, the Joshua tree, is synonymous with the Mojave Desert to travelers and western movie fans alike.

The Chihuahuan Desert, which occupies a relatively small area of southern New Mexico and the Texas panhandle but drives a wedge through the heart of northern Mexico, is North America's largest desert. The tall, columnar, often many-armed saguaro cactus looms large on the horizon of the Sonoran Desert of western Mexico, Arizona, and extreme southeastern California. Southern California, from the foothills of the Sierra Nevada to the Pacific Ocean, is dominated by chaparral, a dense scrubland characterized by as few as one or as many as twenty different evergreen shrub species, including the heatherlike *Adenostoma fasciculatum* or greasewood, various manzanitas (*Arctostaphylos* species), and *Ceanothus*, or wild lilac. Chaparral typically develops in so-called Mediterranean regions with mild, wet winters and very dry summers.

Today most ecologists believe that Frederic Clements went off the deep end when he theorized that plant communities were integrated units, and as such were somehow greater than the sum of their parts—much as organisms are greater than the sum of their cells, tissues, and organs. They point out that plant associations, unlike organisms, often do not have well-defined boundaries, and that changes in species composition and abundance occur gradually. Still, there are recognizable differences between, for example, the tallgrass and shortgrass prairies, and the association concept is useful not only for botanists but also for gardeners trying to determine which communities of plants are native to their areas.

So if you live, as I do, in the oak-chestnut association in the eastern deciduous forest formation, and you're interested in designing your garden for maximum diversity by preserving ecosystem structure, then you'd do well to make a woodland garden the core of your landscape. It doesn't have to be a totally native woodland garden. Recent books on natural gardening have confused preservation of the *structure* of a natural community with compilation of a list of native species to plant, but they're not necessarily the same thing. The application of natural models in the garden doesn't always have to be literal, though I'm all for planting natives unless there's a good reason not to, since indigenous species have lost—and continue to lose—so much ground. And sometimes it can make sense to re-create a native plant community down to the smallest possible detail. Our woodland garden on Shelter Island is a good example. The property is contiguous with a larger expanse of forest, albeit one that is but a shrunken fragment of the once-awesome forest canopy that used to cover virtually the entire island, rimmed by sandy dunes and broken only occasionally by bays, tidal creeks, and salt marshes. Here, aside from the odd potted exotic nectar plant to draw butterflies, I've planted exclusively native species to augment the slender sliver of forest that is the largest tract of wild woodland remaining on Shelter Island's West Neck. In front of the house, we're helping what was a struggling lawn revert back to forest: simply by replacing the leaf litter, we've encouraged acorns to grow into small oak saplings, and sassafras is colonizing the open understory, while whorled loosestrife (*Lysimachia quadrifolia*), with its dainty yellow early-summer flowers, is sweeping across the forest floor. Someday I'll get around to adding a few shad and dogwood, restoring the highbush blueberries that dominate the shrub layer in the local woodlands, and reestablishing a greater diversity of wildflowers and ferns. I've planted glades of native lady, cinnamon, sensitive, and interrupted ferns instead of traditional foundation plantings, and have coaxed small patches of moss to become a velvety lawn in the tiny clearing around the house.

Sometimes it may suffice to mimic the overall vegetation type while employing at least some nonnative species as "functional analogues" of the native plants. In a garden that acts like nature, restoring ecological structure and process is more important than choosing species from a native-plants list. However, it must be admitted that intelligent selection of a functional analogue of a native plant is easier said than done, simply because there's still so much we don't know about what role individual species play in their natural communities. Some plants obviously have important functions—a canopy tree in a forest, for instance. If you're looking for a workable substitute, you'd better opt for another canopy species and not, say, a shrub, or you'll drastically alter the character of the community. If prairie is your natural model and you're searching for a stand-in for wild lupine, you'd be best off picking another nitrogen-fixing leguminous herb to help maintain the fertility of the soil. But bear in mind that your new arrangement may prove detrimental to some poor pollinator or other creature dependent upon the native canopy tree or the lupine.

Our Brooklyn neighborhood has been so hacked to pieces by asphalt, concrete, and brick that as an ecosystem it is severely dysfunctional, to say the least. Here, too, we've created a woodland garden, but in this case one that only alludes to the rich morainal oak forests that once blanketed the area. It, too, is

Sweet pepperbush
(Clethra alnifolia).

composed of mostly native plants, chosen for the benefit of the birds and other creatures that must eke out an existence in the inner city. But I've been far from purist in my approach, planting sweet pepperbush—native to Brooklyn wetlands but not to the drier upland habitat in our backyard—because butterflies, bees, and other insects love its fragrant white spikes of late-summer flowers, as do I. Since one of the main functions of an urban garden is to provide a soothing retreat from the hustle and bustle and sometimes the discord of city life, I've planted *Campsis radicans* 'Flava', a yellow-flowered form of the native trumpet vine— to lure hummingbirds, yes, but mostly, I confess, because it harmonizes with the creamy whites, pale yellows, and blues that create a calming effect in the garden, something the bright-red flowers of the species proper definitely wouldn't do. *Campsis* is native to our neck of the woods—it grows vigorously in nearby Prospect Park—but I haven't the foggiest idea where the cultivar 'Flava' comes from. Then, too, I've spared the old nonnative sweet autumn clematis vine, which certainly would garner no oohs and aahs on the garden-tour circuit but is nonetheless most appreciated by the small flocks of juncos that dine on its fluffy seedheads in the dead of winter. I've also added loads of cheery early-spring-flowering bulbs that dispel the winter blahs—not only mine but also, I like to think, those of any hapless pollinators stymied by the slim pickings of that season.

At times the application of a natural model can be quite abstract. Dr. Bill Wolverton, an environmental scientist who pioneered natural approaches to sewage treatment in the early 1970s while at NASA, has developed artificial rock-bed "marshes" that are now treating sewage in private yards in Louisiana, Mississippi, Alabama, and other southern states. These mini-marshes consist of a trench lined with a plastic membrane and filled to a depth of twelve inches or so with river rock capped with pea gravel. The wastewater never rises above the river rock, plants are transplanted into the pea-gravel layer, and their roots grow down into the river-rock zone. Pollutants in the wastewater are broken down by microorganisms and become food for the plants. These marshes can be planted with cattails, bulrushes, and other native wetland species, or with cannas, calla lilies, irises, ginger lilies, elephant ears, or other ornamentals. They often bear only the most superficial resemblance to natural wetlands, and yet they successfully carry out one of the most valuable ecological processes of wetland ecosystems: the assimilation of pollutants.

AS CLEMENTS CRISSCROSSED the country with Edith behind the wheel, he observed that vegetation type wasn't the only way that plant communities exhibited structure. Plant life is organized into vertical layers, or strata, which are most obvious in forests but may be found in virtually all plant communities. Below the woodland canopy, small trees, shrubs, herbs, ferns, and mosses comprise at least three distinct layers of foliage. Small trees form the understory; shrubs and sapling trees make up the shrub layer; and wildflowers, ferns, and mosses create a tapestry known as the ground layer. The vertical layers are not just above-ground; they also extend down among the roots. In the American prairie, for instance, big and little bluestem and other fibrous-rooted grasses dominate the upper layers of the soil, leaving plenty of room for deep-rooted forbs such as butterfly weed.

According to current evolutionary theory, species within a community are driven to partition the environment—that is, to utilize different parts of it, such as the various vertical layers. This minimizes the competition that always occurs where two or more plants require limited resources such as light, nutrients, or water. Competition is greatest between those individuals or species that make similar demands upon the same resources at the same time—meaning it is more intense between closely related species (as, for example, between a grass and a grass), than between more distant relatives (e.g., a grass and a deep-rooted forb).

Traditionally, the gardener's chief concern (though it generally hasn't been recognized as such) has been to regulate the kind and degree of competition among his or her plants, usually through weed control. The concept of vertical structure offers a new way to think about competition in an age of extinction. By choosing plants to fill all the available layers in our gardens, we not only leave little room for weeds but also boost biodiversity, because in general, the greater the number of distinctive vertical strata in a community, the more diverse the plant life, and therefore the more habitat provided for a more diverse array of animal life.

Plant communities also exhibit a kind of horizontal structure that's more familiar to conscientious gardeners. Practically all vegetation will show more or less striking differences virtually every few feet. Variations in the physical environment—here a little drier, perhaps due to thinner soil or a gentle slope, there a little wetter because of a slight depression—will be reflected in both the number and kinds of plants present, producing a patchwork or mosaic of different habitats across the landscape. To gardeners, these differences are more commonly known as microclimates. Ecologically minded gardeners can use this rich, complex system of patterns within the larger vegetation pattern as still another model for an equally rich and biodiverse garden design. The dry, sunny slope may thus afford an opportunity to create a grassland garden of drought-loving prairie or meadow plants, while the moist depression may offer a site for a wetland garden.

There's yet another important aspect of vegetation structure: it changes with the seasons. Especially in temperate climates where the seasons are quite distinct, different species in any particular plant association will grow most vigorously, flower, and fruit at different times during the growing season. Clements termed these seasonal variations in structure "aspects." They're just one more way that nature manages to cram as much biodiversity as possible into any given plot of land.

In much of the eastern deciduous forest, as the days lengthen and spring sunshine pours through the bare tree branches and warms the ground, an explosion of growth begins. The forest floor is transformed into a spectacular carpet of ephemeral wildflowers. Soon, tree buds break, and the burst of leaf growth begins to form a veil of shade. By the time the canopy closes in, most of the wildflowers have disappeared, and the woodland floor is a study in greens: ferns, mosses, and the foliage of herbaceous plants. Then, as summer wanes, the forest blossoms anew with asters, goldenrods, and grasses. These late blooms are accompanied by a profusion of ripening berries. The rich golds, fiery reds, and bright blues portend the autumnal foliage spectacle to come.

Here's how Clements described the seasonal aspects of the shortgrass prairie of his native Nebraska:

> Certain sedges (*Carex*), prairie cat's foot (*Antennaria*), and prairie windflower (*Anemone*) stand out conspicuously during April against the brown background of dry grasses and herbs. They constitute the early spring or prevernal aspect. During May, the purple and blue of societies of ground plum (*Astragalus*), the massive cream-colored racemes of falso indigo (*Baptisia*), and the bright yellow heads of *Senecio*, with many other spring or vernal societies, add tone to the landscape. But by June most of these have waned and the prairies until late July are characterized by extensive summer or estival societies of many-flowered psoralea (*Psoralea*), daisies (*Erigeron*), . . . lead plant (*Amorpha*), rose, and many others. Then, again, the scenes are shifted. The purple of the autumnal societies of blazing stars (*Liatris*) is mixed with the

yellows of goldenrods (*Solidago*) and sunflowers (*Helianthus*). These with the asters and numerous other species mark the end of the growing season.

Even the most skillful gardener would be hard pressed to create a succession of bloom of such duration, subtlety, and refinement.

For gardeners, orchestrating a long-lasting sequence of blooms has traditionally been almost purely a question of aesthetics—a matter of combining flowers in just the right shades of gold and blue, of placing the taller plants at the back of the border and the diminutive ones in the front, of making sure that the next spurt of growth will obscure the previous wave's spent flowers and yellowing foliage. I am suggesting here not that such painterly considerations should have no place in the ecological garden, just that the pictorial sense should be grounded in the larger, natural context. In our Shelter Island garden, for example, a grove of native white-barked birch, *Betula populifolia*, like the one I've often admired in the nearby Nature Conservancy preserve, would enhance the sense of place, while a red-leafed Japanese maple would stick out like a sore thumb.

And not many of us gardeners consider the myriad interactions between the changing spectacle of plants and the creatures that eat them, pollinate them, or disseminate their seeds—still another way that vegetation structure manifests biological diversity. Few, if any, horticultural texts note that the flowering of the woodland wildflower Dutchman's-breeches is timed to the appearance of queen bees, or that box turtles spread the seeds of another denizen of the Northeast's deciduous forests, the quirky mayapple. Gardening books rarely tell us that prairie goldenrods are not only great nectar plants for butterflies but also an important food source for birds foraging in late summer and autumn, or that New Jersey tea, another native of prairie and meadow, is pollinated by flies, which are in turn devoured by hummingbirds.

For a time, Henry Art, a professor of ecology at Williams

College in Massachusetts, was puzzled by the fact that some New England forests have rich herbaceous layers, while in otherwise similar forests the ground layer is depauperate. His research eventually revealed that most of the missing plants, such as trilliums, bloodroot, Dutchman's-breeches, and spring-beauty, are ant-disseminated and have not been able to move far beyond the fragmented islands of undisturbed vegetation; apparently, roads and other development have prevented the ants that disperse the seeds from reaching the second-growth forests that have become so common in the region over the past hundred years. If these wildflowers are to grace the woodland floors of New England's returning forests in spring, gardeners may have to plant them. The same holds for other plants and other gardeners in other regions.

DURING HIS CROSS-CONTINENTAL forays, Frederic Clements noticed that the variety of plant communities in an area was sometimes the result of change in the underlying environment, and at other times a normal process of developmental change, technically referred to as ecological succession. Succession is a predictable variation in community structure over time, toward the highest vegetation type that a particular habitat can support, given the current climate. As the vegetation develops, the area is occupied successively by different plant communities—hence the term "succession." Most succession occurs in areas affected by some kind of disturbance, such as wind-blown gaps in forests or grasslands swept by fire.

When farmland or, better yet, lawn is cleared of all vegetation, the first plants to colonize the area are physiologically tough, aggressive annuals such as horseweed and common ragweed. Within a few years, biennials, many of them nonnative species such as common mullein and Queen-Anne's-lace, will move in, along with a few wildflowers such as asters and goldenrods. In the struggle for light, water, and nutrients that follows,

Ants disseminating the seeds of bloodroot
(Sanguinaria canadensis).

the annuals, which must start anew each year, will begin to disappear, while the perennials, which constantly hold their ground and extend their turf, increase in importance.

In the Great Plains, a disturbed area will pass through these various stages and after many years be populated with buffalo and grama grass and their associated forbs. In the eastern forests, a grassland phase will be followed by "old field," a blend of herbaceous plants, shrubs, and seedlings of such species as maple, ash, dogwood, cherry, pine, and eastern red cedar. As the trees mature, they shade out the sun-loving grasses, wildflowers, evergreens, and shrubs, and the land reverts back to the woodland whence it came. In western Washington and the mountains of Colorado, the final vegetation is coniferous forest.

As an area progresses through the phases of succession, called seral stages, the community biomass, or total living matter, both plant and animal, builds. Organic matter also accumulates, and the soils become richer. Nutrient cycles, meanwhile, become ever more closed, meaning that more nutrients are retained and recycled within the community. The species present during each seral stage change, too. Diversity generally increases.

Consider why succession is such an important process for gardeners to understand: conventional gardening commonly results in substantial disturbance, defined, in an ecological sense, as any activity that causes changes in a natural community, its plant populations, or the soil, including the level of nutrients. When we cultivate the soil, we're creating disturbance. The same goes for when we remove plants, or fertilize. Disturbance creates opportunities for other plants to become established—and the fiercest competitors are often weeds. In other words, when we do many of the things that we've always assumed gardeners are supposed to do, we're encouraging the natural process of succession. It helps to understand this process so we're not constantly fighting it blindly.

But succession is much more than just a pesky process we need to recognize and become resigned to; it can be one of the most creative tools available to garden designers. In the words of biologist John Todd and his wife, the writer Nancy Jack Todd, "Succession is a powerful conceptual tool for thinking about, designing, even reshaping communities. It allows us to cope creatively with change and even to steer it." In the garden, this may mean accelerating the natural process of succession by skipping over entire seral stages—for instance, restoring trees and their associated vegetation instead of waiting out the lengthy annual, perennial, and old-field phases. Jump-starting succession also speeds up its accompanying increase in diversity, from a few simple organisms to a plethora of highly evolved species in complex associations. The Todds put it eloquently: "Such diversity increases the number and, more importantly, the kinds of relationships. . . . This ordered complexity embodies harmony and beauty."

On occasion, it may also make sense to freeze or reverse succession. In some ways we humans have created a kind of passive disturbance by interfering with natural disturbance events that may be critical to the health and even the survival of some plant communities. By extinguishing wildfires in the Midwest and Great Plains, for example, we've enabled woody vegetation to encroach on once-vast grassland ecosystems, which for thousands of years had been periodically enveloped in flames. Horticultural techniques such as mowing and controlled burning can simulate the natural fire regime and discourage or even eliminate undesirable trees and shrubs.

In recent decades, ecologists have come to realize that succession and disturbance foster diversity on a larger scale as well. Biodiversity implies not only a diversity of species but also a diversity of ecosystems. Diversity on a regional level appears to require occasional random disturbance: the most diverse landscapes are composed of a mosaic of patches in various stages of succession, all disturbed at various times in the past by wind throw, fire, disease, or insects. Disturbance ensures the presence and survival of the plants and animals that characterize each successional phase. This, too, can be a model for gardeners. A healthy garden ecosystem not only preserves populations of native species, but also may include representatives of several native ecosystems—woodland, wetland, grassland, scrubland—in a variety of successional states. For a Brooklyn Botanic Garden handbook on biodiversity in the home landscape, designer Gayle Weinstein created a blueprint for a one-acre garden in Colorado that incorporates five of the state's major plant communities: coniferous forest; shorter, more open pygmy forest dominated by piñon pine and single-seed juniper; successional shrubland where wildlife flock to thickets of American plum, scrub oak, and sumac; midgrass and shortgrass prairie; and a stream-side wetland. In the immediate vicinity of the house is a low-maintenance lawn consisting of two native grasses, buffalo grass and blue grama grass.

A FEW YEARS ago, in the mail-order catalog Seeds of Change, Peter Bahouth provided an ecological accounting of the typical North American supermarket-bought tomato. Here's an abbreviated version: The tomato was grown in Mexico from a hybrid seed patented by a genetic-engineering firm. The farm was fumigated with methyl-bromide, one of the most ozone-depleting chemicals in existence, then doused with toxic pesticides; the toxic byproducts of manufacturing the pesticide ended up in the world's largest toxic waste dump, in Alabama. The tomato was packaged in a plastic tray covered with plastic wrap, and placed in a cardboard box. The plastic was manufactured with chlorine, a process that produces extremely toxic byproducts, in Point Comfort, Texas, while the cardboard originated in an old-growth forest in British Columbia, was manufactured in the Great Lakes, and was then shipped to the Mexican farm. The entire process was fueled by oil from the Gulf of Campeche, Mexico. The packaged tomatoes were artificially ripened through the application of ethylene, then transported in refrigerated trucks cooled by ozone-depleting hydrochlorofluorocarbons to consumers throughout North America. At several points in the process, workers and nearby residents risked potentially harmful health effects through exposure to various toxins. And needless to say, a tomato thus produced doesn't offer much in the way of flavor, especially when compared to a mouth-watering 'Brandywine' tomato grown organically in the backyard.

As authors Van der Ryn and Cowan have so neatly put it, the most ecologically benign human designs are those that "make the most active use of life's own patterns of health." Herbert Bormann and Gene Likens described in their studies of New Hampshire's Hubbard Brook forest how terrestrial plants rely for their survival on the flow of energy and water and on the circulation of water, nutrients, and all the other necessities of life through an ecosystem. Called the biogeochemical cycle, this circulation and continual cycling of materials is one of an ecosystem's most important functions.

Every landscape, whether domesticated or wild, receives a new infusion of energy from the sun every day. This energy then undergoes a series of transformations, one of the most fascinating of which is photosynthesis. Photosynthesis fixes the solar energy into living matter, which then makes its way through the food web, supplying all living creatures with energy in turn. The flow of energy is one-way and noncyclic: it is continually being replaced by the sun and lost from the ecosystem, mostly in the form of heat. However, because the amount of water and nutrients in the biosphere is finite, these materials are constantly recycled. Some material does move out of an ecosystem, more so in early than in late stages of succession, but the cycling of nutrients within a natural community is an order of magnitude higher than the movement into and out of it.

Since the beginning of the Industrial Age, we gardeners have flouted the biogeochemical cycle by drawing on materials accumulated over eons and stored within the Earth. We lavish on our landscapes fertilizers synthesized from fossil fuels that date back to the days of the dinosaurs, and in many areas soak them with well water, most of which has been stored in underground aquifers since the Ice Age. The ecological garden, in contrast, works *within* existing water and nutrient cycles, using only as much as can be replaced naturally on the site itself.

One of the characteristics of the nutrient cycle that gardeners can easily mimic is decomposition. In nature, everything produced in the landscape returns to the landscape: fall leaves and branches and other natural detritus are transformed into food for vast populations of decomposing organisms, including bacteria, fungi, numerous species of insects, and worms. In terrestrial ecosystems, decomposition generally occurs in the upper soil layers, where organic materials are converted into inorganic substances that are then released in the ecosystem to be taken up by other organisms as nutrients. Decomposition is the basic process that revitalizes the Earth.

Decomposition can be put to good use in the garden. On land where the topsoil has been scraped away by bulldozers or eroded away by wind or water, an ecologically rich and diverse soil can be re-created via backyard composting of food scraps and garden clippings. More adventurous gardeners will find that composted sewage sludge is even richer in nutrients and can make a fine soil amendment. Compost not only can help restore degraded soil, but also should be applied regularly even to better-endowed lands that are intensively cultivated for vegetables or other crops. It helps rehabilitate "source" landscapes such as gardens while eliminating the need for "sinks" such as garbage dumps.

Gardeners can mimic nature's thrift in yet another way: by conserving water. A native plant community makes do with the water that's available on-site; it doesn't depend on supplies piped in from underground or from hundreds of miles away. Granted, given our current horticultural habits, this degree of water conservation wouldn't be easy, but we can still reduce our consumption by a significant amount. The most obvious way to cut water use is to choose plants better adapted to local precipitation patterns. Even locally adapted transplants need some irrigation for the first year or two, though, and supplemental water is an absolute necessity in the kitchen garden, the container garden, and other highly cultivated areas.

One potential source of supplemental water is runoff from the roof; in fact, most houses used to be equipped with cisterns in the basement or underground to collect every available drop of water. Landscape pioneers can also reclaim the water that exits from natural sewage-treatment systems, such as Bill Wolverton's rock-bed marshes, for use elsewhere in the garden. And the resourceful gardener who has gone to great lengths to capture precious water will have plenty of incentive to distribute it to needy garden denizens via drip irrigation or other water-conserving technology.

Because the discipline of ecology is still in its infancy, we gardeners will be experimenting along with the scientists. For the foreseeable future, gardening will be one part learning to live within our ecological means, and one part art—doing what feels right. The conservationist Aldo Leopold suggested the possibility of a human natural aesthetic when he defined "right" as anything that "tends to preserve the beauty and stability of the biotic community."

In an essay titled "The Self-effacing Art: Restoration as Imitation of Nature," Frederick Turner has described recent research on the biological foundation of aesthetics. This new research suggests that our aesthetic sense is in essence a capacity to make sense of masses of amorphous information and to perceive harmonies in them that add up to a deep unity. This unity generates predictions for the future and can act as a sound basis for future actions. Our efforts are rewarded and reinforced by the experience of aesthetic pleasure. In other words, if we gardeners will only open our eyes to nature, our aesthetic sense will help us do what's right.

Gardens within the Garden

THE PAST FEW decades have given rise to a remarkable series of challenges to conventional gardening's techniques and tools, as well as to its style and philosophy. In the 1960s and '70s, as evidence of the health and ecological dangers of pesticides began piling up, organic gardening gained ground. More recently, as it has become clearer that plants and animals are rapidly disappearing from our land and our lives, there has been an increasing interest in planting native species.

We stand at the threshold of a new iteration of ecological garden design, one whose concerns and goals are deeper, more coherent, and more complex than simply swearing *off* chemicals and swearing *by* wildflowers. What does it borrow from traditional gardening? How do the horticultural movements of recent years fit in? What does a garden that acts like nature *look* like? The only way to answer these questions is to flesh out a vision of the future garden.

An ecological garden is one that includes plantings that

honor our own species's long and fruitful relationship with the land, whether an elegant herb garden accented with topiary spirals or a patio edged with fragrant flower borders. There's certainly a place in the garden for healthy, home-grown food. An ecological landscape design makes the natural processes of decay and renewal visible, celebrating nature's inherent thrift. It performs the vital task of restoring the rich ecology of the natural landscape, whether it's a lush hardwood hammock in subtropical Florida or a sea of prairie wildflowers and grasses in the upper Midwest. What's more, by blurring the sharp edges between indoors and outdoors, it tells a story about the fundamental unity between humanity and the rest of nature. The result is a diversity of species in a variety of habitats—or, in more traditional gardening terms, a number of gardens *within* the garden.

The Garden Room

For years, like most other American gardeners, I oohed and aahed over English garden rooms, especially the ones in those magnificent, turn-of-the-century country-house spreads designed by architect Edwin Lutyens and plantswoman Gertrude Jekyll. The grass always looks greener in the other guy's yard, I guess. It wasn't until I started writing about old houses here in North America that I realized that the garden room has flowered most profusely on this side of the Atlantic. In the hands of Americans, it has become both a horticultural showplace and a down-to-earth living space. The outdoor living room is this country's greatest contribution to the history of landscape design, and doubtless will remain an important feature of gardens yet to come.

Something about being American makes most of us want to live close to nature. Every grade-school tyke hears the story of how, in March 1845, Henry David Thoreau began his experiment on an uninhabited tract of land on Walden Pond, near Concord, Massachusetts. "I went to the woods," he later wrote in *Walden*, "because I wished to live deliberately, to front only the essential facts of life, and see if I could not learn what it had to teach, and not, when I came to die, discover that I had not lived."

Most of Thoreau's contemporaries were too busy carving up the wilderness to be particularly concerned about communing with it. But as the nineteenth century wore on and sprawling cities and smoke-belching factories began obliterating more and more of the natural landscape, many Americans began to yearn for a more pastoral life. By the end of the century, the pioneers of American design were rebelling against Victorian artifice and its ostentatious trappings of industrialism, especially its overly elaborate machine-made ornament- and cookie-cutter-shaped flower beds. They turned to nature for inspiration, and American landscape architects have been moving toward a marriage of structure and nature ever since.

Around the same time that Lutyens and Jekyll were producing their masterpieces, Gustav Stickley, a maker of Mission-style furniture, launched a new magazine called *The Craftsman* and brought a new naturalism in both home and landscape design to the American middle class. Stickley waxed eloquent on the relationship between architecture and nature: "Whatever connects a house with out of doors, whether vines or flowers, piazza or pergola," he wrote, "it is to be welcomed in the scheme of modern home-making. We need outdoor life in this country; we need it inherently, because it is the normal thing for all people, and we need it specifically as a nation, because we are an overwrought people, too eager about everything except peace and contentment."

This bit of *Craftsman* philosophy was embedded in an article championing pergolas in American gardens. Stickley believed that the pergola—an arbor formed by a double row of posts or pillars with joists above, and the whole covered with climbing plants—"epitomizes modern outdoor life, and its beauty [lies in its] simplicity of construction and intimacy with Nature." Every garden, he insisted, must have such a living room outdoors, one "draped in vines, that gives us green walls to live within, that has a ceiling of tangled leaves and flowers blowing in the wind, a glimpse of blue sky through open spaces, and sunshine pouring over us when the leaves move."

From 1901 until 1916, when it ceased publication, *The Craftsman* provided designs for simple farmhouses with pergolas, suburban stucco houses with wraparound pergolas, and bungalows with pergolas framing the approach to the front door. There were picturesque pergolas, featuring cobblestone piers topped with rustic poles, and classical pergolas with turned wooden columns, plain or fluted, and trellised roofs. Stickley instructed his readers to choose their materials from the local landscape, whether fieldstone or terra cotta, white pine or madrone, so that the outdoor room would harmonize with nature.

Turn-of-the-century designers did not stop with the pergola in their quest to link nature with daily life: porches, courtyards, and terraces were also furnished as outdoor living rooms. Open-air dining rooms were much admired and sometimes came complete with a fireplace that shared a chimney with the kitchen range indoors. Just as important was the "sleeping porch." Post-Victorians believed that fresh air was as important to the body as fragrant bowers, the songs of birds, and a sky spangled with stars were to the spirit, and many period houses included one or more sleeping porches near the bedrooms on the first or second floor.

One home design published in *The Craftsman* in 1909, billed as a "House with Court, Pergolas, Outdoor Living Rooms, and Sleeping Balconies," combined all of these most desired features. A broad terrace runs across the front of the house and continues around the side, where it becomes a porch meant to be used as an outdoor living room. The kitchen shares a chimney with a fireplace on the back porch. From there, steps lead down into a courtyard surrounded by a sun-splashed, vine-festooned pergola. Upstairs is an outdoor sleeping room. This house was meant to foster outdoor life in a mild climate such as California's. Already, California had established its reputation as a place where there was a certain feeling of unity between house and garden, where the outdoors was simply an extension of the home. "Living so much out of doors," Stickley, a New Jersey resident, wrote somewhat wistfully, "Californians almost instinctively make the transition between outdoors and indoors as little marked as possible."

OUR NEED FOR nature and the "outdoor life," as Gustav Stickley put it, has become ever more urgent since the early decades of this century. Thanks to Californian Thomas Church and a handful of other pioneers of the modern movement in landscape design during the 1930s, '40s, and '50s, the garden room has become firmly ensconced in the routines of daily life. It has become a place to relax with a book, to dine alfresco, to lounge around the pool, or to host a weekend barbecue. Today, several decades into modernism, the typical garden has become smaller, the pace of life faster, and the outdoor room ever more important as a middle ground, a link, between domesticity and wilderness.

The outdoor room honors the glorious history of the garden, whether with lush herbaceous borders, an *allée* of pleached pears, or fragrant roses for cutting. A few years ago, when I was researching a book on ecological house and garden design, I saw an unforgettable home situated on a small parcel of land near the southern California coast. Each room in the pink stucco house had French doors that opened onto a different garden room. One bedroom led to a quaint parterre garden where gray and green santolina were planted in alternating squares, like a billowy checkerboard carpet; across the parterre garden from the French doors, a handsome wooden bench was placed along a hedge of evergreen Greek myrtle, flanked by lemon trees in terra-cotta pots. The indoor dining room spilled out onto a pic-turesque courtyard enclosed on two sides by the house's walls and screened from the street by a pink-washed stucco wall. The wall itself was topped by a pergola over which was draped a magnifi-cent native Dutchman's pine vine. The courtyard was as cozy as any indoor room, with a tile floor, chairs and skirted tables, pots overflowing with fragrant herbs and flowers, and a fireplace for cooking as well as for warmth on chilly desert evenings. Only one garden room had no entry from the house. A hidden path led to this secret place, where a diminutive wetland garden could be contemplated from a nicely weathered old stone bench.

The outdoor room celebrates not only our own relationship with the land but also our essential oneness with the rest of nature. It actually comprises a series of gardens designed to ease the transition from cultivated to wild. If the Eskimos, as has often been noted, have a dozen words for "snow," late-twentieth-century Americans have at least that many for the spaces that ease the transition from human habitation to natural habitat: porch, pergola, patio, arbor, balcony, terrace, veranda, deck, court-yard, gallery, gazebo, garden room. Each expresses an exquisitely subtle distinction in the degree of progression from inside to outdoors. The porch, for example, which first appeared in nineteenth-century America, is usually covered by a roof and often partially surrounded by walls, and therefore is closely asso-ciated with the house. It is furnished with upholstered chairs, tables draped in linen or chintz, freshly cut flowers, and all the luxuries of civilization. The post-Victorian pergola, in contrast, with its ceiling of joists and tangled leaves and flowers, is truly a transitional space; framing the entrance to the house, it quite poetically leads from darkness to light. A mid-twentieth-century patio gives merely a suggestion of enclosed space and is thus more closely associated with nature. A "floor" of clipped lawn or fieldstone and thyme may be all that distinguishes it as living space. The late-twentieth-century garden room may in fact be defined by nothing more than the furniture it holds: a rustic wooden bench under the boughs of an ancient bur oak surrounded by wild prairie, for instance, or a twig chair in a small clearing in a forest.

I tend to garden on the wild side. Our Shelter Island living room opens through double glass doors onto a screened porch surrounded by glades of fern. The porch leads to an outdoor patio where Don and I barbecue and picnic all summer long. Among our favorite visitors are butterflies, some of nature's loveliest pollinators; the patio brushes up against the butterfly garden I planted at the edge of the surrounding coastal forest.

In keeping with the wild character of the site, the butterfly garden is really more of a meadow, dominated by little bluestem, whose bluish hues turn russet in autumn, and Indian grass, whose late-summer blooms become small, brown nutlet seeds that eventually form attractive plumes. In early spring, the meadow is a wash of pastel purple when the bird's-foot violet blooms; this exquisite, large-flowered violet of Long Island's pine barrens, sporting ragged-edged leaves that look like a bird's footprints, was once very common but has become rare as its habitat has disappeared. Throughout the garden, the color of the violets is echoed by the iridescent flashes of Spring Azures and Eastern Tailed Blues, tiny but beautiful creatures that provide some of the first signs of butterfly activity in the spring. Summer brings the brilliant orange-flowered butterfly weed, which never fails to live up to its name. The butterflies don't stop coming until late October, when the last asters and goldenrods have gone to seed.

On the other side of the patio, the butterfly garden continues in a dampish area that we've transformed into a backyard bog. Here a border of wetland bloomers, including Joe-pye weed (which waves its eight-foot-tall, butterfly-laden flowerheads for weeks in late summer), dusty rose-flowered swamp milkweed, and sweet pepperbush, with its fragrant spires of white flowers, lure even more beautiful pollinators.

Each season some new species comes to sip nectar from the flowers that nod their heads next to our picnic table. One year, Silver-Spotted Skippers and Question Marks discovered the miniature meadow; the next, the Tiger Swallowtail and the bright-yellow Clouded Sulphur made an appearance.

Food plants for butterfly larvae are not necessarily the same as nectar plants for adults. In the woods that cover most of our property grow many of the plants favored by the caterpillars: sassafras, wild cherry, birch, blueberry, dogwood.

Now I'm trying to become better acquainted with the butterflies' close relatives the moths. These poor critters have gotten a bum rap: they don't *all* eat their way through priceless woollens. Butterflies, which get all the good press, account for only about 765 of the more than 11,000 species of the order Lepidoptera that are found north of the Mexican border; the other ten-thousand-plus are moths.

Many moths are quite beautiful. They don't come just in shades of mousey gray; some have spots, bands of color, and graceful shapes to rival those of any butterfly. Some, like butterflies, sip nectar from flowers. A moth-pollinated flower is often tubelike in construction to accommodate the creature's long proboscis or tongue (incredibly, some moths have tongues a full foot long).

A few moths, I've discovered, fly by day—the Hummingbird moth, for example, which I once mistook for its avian namesake. There it was, hovering above a clump of bee balm, its wings flapping and vibrating, before suddenly dashing away to another flower. Somewhat smaller than an actual hummingbird, this moth frequently touches down on the flowers it visits, and may even crawl over them in a distinctly beelike way. A close relative of the Hummingbird moth, the Bumblebee Clearwing, really looks like a large bumblebee.

Ever since I was a kid I've been fascinated by the night-flying moths that press up against screens and windows, drawn to the

The Luna moth on a birch branch.

light. Night-flying species are not likely to reveal themselves as easily as butterflies—which is too bad, since they include some of the largest and most beautiful of moths. Nocturnal moths rarely leave their daytime hideouts until dusk, that magical time when colors blur and familiar shapes become mysterious. All night long, as they flit from flower to flower or search for mates, they remain cloaked by the cover of darkness.

One of the most elegant night-flying species is the sea-green Luna, a giant silk moth with a four-inch wingspan measured from tip to tip of its showy forewings, and hind wings that taper off into long, streamerlike tails. At dawn, the adult luna flattens itself against a limb or tree trunk, and there it remains, motionless, until darkness falls.

There's a world of difference between flowers that bloom during the day and those that open at night. Not surprisingly, flowers that lure butterflies and other insects that fly by day rely on visual appeal and typically come in bright colors. Those that attract nocturnal moths are usually either glowing white or the palest yellow, and give off a strong perfume. The fragrance of some of these flowers is so intense, in fact, that it can be detected from great distances by the moths that pollinate them.

I have some homework to do. Many of the plants recommended for moth fanciers are nonnative; some, such as honeysuckle and purple loosestrife, are quite invasive. Over the next few years, I'll be looking for night-blooming flowers that are indigenous or at least ecologically benign to grow in pots in our Shelter Island garden room. But that's part of the charm of gardening with nature—the constant experimentation and discovery and pleasure that come as new worlds on the periphery of human life unfold.

The Indoor Garden

Around the same time that Gustav Stickley was popularizing porches, pergolas, and other garden rooms, Frank Lloyd Wright was designing what he called the "natural house." Wright declared that the citizens of a democracy deserved to live in something better than a "box"—the kind of dark, claustrophobic residential structure we Americans inherited from the Old World. The natural house, he wrote, would help liberate us from the stale traditions of Europe by awakening in us a "desire for such far-reaching simplicities of life as we may see in the clear countenance of nature." So that we could better see nature, Wright replaced opaque walls with long expanses of clear glass.

As any indoor gardener knows, glass is great stuff, one of the real luxuries of twentieth-century life. One reason Wright was enamored of glass was that truly transparent, fool-the-eye glazing was something new in his day. It wasn't until the middle of the nineteenth century that an even moderately transparent glass became available, replacing the crown glass of the Colonial era, also called bull's-eye glass because of the spiral pattern that showed where the glass had once been attached to the glass-blower's pipe. Even several inches away from the bull's-eye, crown glass was still thick and wavy, and it could be cut only into tiny panes.

Cylinder glass was a Victorian innovation that required a small assembly line of workers. The process began with the usual glassblower's bubble, but instead of blowing the bubble into a wide globe, the blower let it hang down from his pipe and swung it over a pit as he worked, creating an elongated shape. A "gatherer" added additional glass, increasing the size of the cylinder. After the blowpipe was detached, the cylinder was allowed to cool and then slit top to bottom and flattened out with a sort of wooden hoe. The outer surface of the cylinder, which was always larger than the inner one, inevitably wrinkled and puckered as the "ironer" worked; the finished product was more suited to a funhouse than to the natural house.

Early indoor gardeners as well as homeowners had to make do with this primitive material. In eighteenth-century Europe, the first "glasshouses" were used to grow tender plants such as orange trees that could not be cultivated year-round outdoors. In the nineteenth century, greenhouses were often attached to houses, in part so that the beauty and fragrance of flowers could enhance everyday living. Conservatories filled with rare and exotic plants collected from remote corners of the globe were also a status symbol—despite the fact that the glass was slightly wavy.

It took a full-blown industrial revolution to bring about the next innovation in glazing technology: plate glass. Molten glass was poured onto a large iron table, rolled smooth with a large roller, and allowed slowly to cool, until it emerged as a sheet of very hard glass of uniform thickness. Any marks caused by contact with the table and roller were painstakingly ground down and polished, resulting in glass that was brilliantly shiny and almost perfect optically. Plate glass was first produced at a profit in 1883, around the time when Frank Lloyd Wright began designing houses.

Frank Lloyd Wright and the Victorians were lucky: they didn't have to worry about OPEC or the depletion of fossil fuels. If they had, the greenhouse and the natural house never would have been invented. As anyone who lives in the late-twentieth century knows only too well, heat leaks through glass like a sieve and can make any structure, whether of glass or conventionally framed, extremely expensive to heat and cool.

That's why gardeners should start a campaign to canonize Day Chahroudi. Thanks to Chahroudi, who grew up in a Frank Lloyd Wright house in Mahopac, New York, we're fast approaching the day when windows will be as conserving of warmth or cooled air as walls—but better, because they'll enable us to open our cocoonlike shelters to the sunlight, and to share them with a profusion of plants.

In the 1970s, Chahroudi helped develop the first windows with low-E, or low-emissivity, coatings. In low-E glass, an atoms-thin layer of metal, typically applied to one of the panes in a double-glazed window, essentially forms a "mirror" that reflects long-wave infrared energy, the fancy term for heat. The beauty of a low-E coating is that while it will reflect heat, it also lets through most incoming light. In cold areas, heat trying to escape is reflected back into the house by a low-E coating applied on the *inside* of the glass, while in hot climates, a coating on the *outside* of a pane will deflect the sun's warming rays before they can enter the structure. By substituting environmentally safe gases such as argon or krypton for the plain old air between the panes, manufacturers have made low-E windows even more energy-efficient, since these inert gases conduct heat less readily than does air.

While working at a Palo Alto, California, company called Southwall Technologies, Chahroudi perfected a product called Heat Mirror, which is even more energy-conserving than ordinary low-E glass. It consists of a sheet of plastic with one or two low-E coatings that can be stretched between the panes of glass in a window frame. The plastic acts like an additional pane of glass, creating two insulating spaces that can then be filled with argon or krypton gas.

Heat Mirror can be manufactured in a variety of different forms to suit not only different climates but also different expo-sures (and, for the indoor gardener, different plants). Depending on the particular configuration, it can be four or five times as energy-efficient as double-paned glass, or even more. The West-facing windows in my Shelter Island house, for example, would be good candidates for a plastic film with a double low-E coating on one side to keep in warm air in winter, allow in good levels of natural light, and block some of the solar heat from the setting summer sun.

An indoor environment geared primarily to plants will differ in at least one important respect from one geared primarily to people: the amount of light that's optimal. Most flowering plants require a lot more light than people do. Until quite recently, conventional wisdom held that a greenhouse could be designed for either optimum light transmission or energy-efficiency, but not both. In another respect, plants and people are quite similar: most plants, like people, don't appreciate being dragged along on the inevitable thermal roller-coaster ride that occurs daily in greenhouses in most American climates, as winter nighttime temperatures take a thirty- or forty-degree nosedive. In the old days, greenhouse heaters had to run full-blast all winter, with most of the warmth escaping immediately through the glass, while on summer afternoons, the greenhouse would get as hot as a pistol, the tender foliage easily sizzling without some sort of shading device. That's why even today, greenhouse owners often whitewash their roofs in summer, to limit the amount of solar radiation penetrating in.

Not too long ago, it seemed that double glazing was about as good as a greenhouse would ever get, at least as far as energy conservation went. Single glazing transmits about 89 percent of available light, and double glazing about 80 percent; glazing that reduces light transmission below that level does not let in enough light for most flowering plants. The problem is, even ordinary double-paned glass is four or five times less energy-efficient than a wall that's only moderately insulated.

The effects of the various wavelengths of light on plant growth was long one of the great mysteries of plant physiology, and to some extent remains so today. In experiments using lamps that emit only certain portions of the spectrum, scientists have found that red light and blue light have the most significant effect on plants. Together, the two play an important role in photosynthesis. Red light exerts the greatest influence on the formation of chlorophyll (the green pigment essential for transforming sunlight into living matter), on dormancy, and on photoperiodism, the relationship between flowering and the length of day (or, more precisely, night). Blue, meanwhile, is the major trigger for phototropism, or the bending of plants toward light. Of course, things are never quite that cut-and-dried. Sometimes responses to blue light may be modified by red or far-red light, and different plants may react to certain wavelengths in slightly different ways. For example, seed germination in most species appears to be stimulated by red light, but far-red light can also *inhibit* germination in some plants.

To study the effect of Heat Mirror on plants, the University of Arizona's Environmental Research Laboratory tested two forms of the material. One was designed to reflect 42 percent of the shortwave infrared radiation while transmitting 82 percent of what scientists call the photosynthetically active radiation, which, as the term suggests, has a substantial influence on plant growth; the other was designed to reflect 71 percent of the infrared and transmit 71 percent of the visible light required for photosynthesis. These two forms of Heat Mirror were then compared to more conventional greenhouse glazing materials. The effects of the various materials on three ornamental crops— geraniums (*Pelargonium* x *hortorum* 'Mustang'), marigolds (*Tagetes erecta* 'Orange Boy'), and petunias (a hybrid cultivar called 'Red Cascade')—were noted.

As expected, the Heat Mirror films were a lot more effective at reducing energy use than the conventional materials. Surprisingly, however, the Heat Mirror also enhanced plant growth in a number of ways, especially during the winter months. The University of Arizona researchers detected what they called a "dramatic early blooming effect of five to ten days," which they ascribed to the Heat Mirror's reversal of the normal ratio of red to far-red light, as well as to the comfortable thermal environment it created for the plants. There were other surprises, too. The marigold seeds germinated faster and the petunias developed larger stems and more succulent, healthy foliage when grown under Heat Mirror, while the geraniums produced the greatest number of blooms under the version of Heat Mirror that admitted the higher percentage of visible light. In other words, the high-tech glazing technology was not only letting in enough light, but also minimizing temperature stress and the kinds of damaging radiation that can burn leaves.

A substance called Cloud Gel is another Day Chahroudi invention. Cloud Gel is a clear goop designed to be sandwiched between two sheets of plastic suspended between panes of glass in a window frame. It's "smarter" than low-E glazings such as Heat Mirror in that it responds to various temperatures by controlling the amount of light admitted. A specially formulated polymer mixed with water, it turns milky white when the window reaches a specified temperature, thereby blocking out as much as 90 percent of the solar heat. Cloud Gel can be fabricated to turn white at any temperature between 60 and 150 degrees Fahrenheit. Although heat is reflected, light is not, which means that Cloud Gel saves energy that would otherwise have to be used for cooling, even as it keeps temperatures comfortable for plants and blocks potentially damaging infrared and UV radiation. When the temperature cools, Cloud Gel once again becomes transparent. The product is made by Chahroudi's company, Suntek, based in Albuquerque, New Mexico.

IN "NATURAL HOMES" of the past century, the boundary between nature and architecture has been blurred. As Frank Lloyd Wright predicted, the profusion of glass in the modern home has afforded us, as he put it, "something of the freedom of our arboreal ancestors living in their trees." Expanses of glass are now standard fare in the American home, from banks of windows to sliding glass doors to skylights that reveal constellations in the nighttime sky.

Still, the union of nature and architecture that Wright envisioned was ultimately aesthetic and theoretical; the natural house was designed to permit people to view nature passively, through transparent walls. But thanks to new technologies that are allowing us to use ever more glass in our dwellings, the boundary between nature and architecture, between indoors and outdoors, is disappearing entirely. The house itself is becoming a garden.

Like their Victorian predecessors, modern sun-spaces ranging from exquisite English-style conservatories to elegant redwood-and-glass structures enable us to transcend the limits of our climates, to grow, for example, extravagant tropical orchids native to steamy jungles and vapor-shrouded mountain slopes. Serious kitchen gardeners can cultivate an astonishing variety of plants indoors just by designing a greenhouse that includes a number of different microclimates.

During the 1970s, a group of landscape pioneers working with the now-defunct New Alchemy Institute on Cape Cod, Massachusetts, began developing a new, ecological approach to indoor horticulture. They called their new indoor gardens bioshelters. A miniature ecosystem comprising people, animals, and plants, a bioshelter makes it possible to produce a significant amount of food year-round.

Bioshelters can be small or large, elaborate or relatively simple. Like conventional greenhouses, they can be added to the south side of a house. The major difference between a bioshelter and an ordinary greenhouse is that the former is both biologically diverse and ecologically balanced.

A bioshelter provides the indoor living spaces with solar heat as it supplies fresh, pesticide-free food throughout the winter months. Inside the indoor garden are raised not only vegetables and fruits but also fish, which live in water-filled translucent tanks about three feet in diameter. The fish subsist on the algae that forms in the solar tanks, and in turn fertilize the lettuce, watercress, or other plants that grow rafted on the surface. Outside the bioshelter, a variety of plants offer shade, flowers, food, or fragrance in the warmer months.

Bioshelters are designed for thermal mass—that is, to retain solar heat. Different kinds of thermal storage add to the structure's energy efficiency and provide for the many microclimates that nurture the bioshelter's diverse animals and plants. A high masonry north wall, for instance, creates a vertical warm zone for climbing and espaliered plants such as grapes and figs. Raised masonry beds on different levels create more microclimates; those closest to the glass may be used to grow spinach and other cool-weather crops.

The water in the tanks used for indoor aquaculture is another source of thermal mass; the above-ground "ponds" are particularly good at absorbing low-angle winter sunlight. The soil itself is still another means of thermal storage. Rather than being planted in pots, plants in a bioshelter are typically set in soil that is separated from the earth outside by insulated walls that extend below the frost line. This not only provides thermal mass but also enhances the biological diversity of the mini-ecosystem, making it more hospitable to earthworms and a variety of soil organisms. What's more, it allows small fruit trees or other woody plants with sizable root systems to be included in the bioshelter.

Homes of the not-too-distant future will feature yet another Day Chahroudi innovation dubbed the Weather Panel, a transparent "skin" that can capture even the weak light emitted by winter clouds—called cloudlight—and that may replace the conventional opaque roof. Instead of an attic, homes will have a bioshelter on the top floor. Weather Panels combine a low-E coating with Cloud Gel in prefabricated roof panels. The shade provided by potted trees and planters hanging from the ceiling eliminates glare in the sun-space—thereby making for a pleasant living room, dining room, or kitchen. Alternatively, these rooms can be in their traditional, ground-floor location, freeing the sun-space to serve as a year-round tropical garden and indoor gazebo.

In a much more radical departure, in the twenty-first century home, not only conventional food plants and houseplants but also ecological communities once confined to the outdoors will be able to live within the house's walls.

I got my first glimpse of a true twenty-first century home—or at least the blueprints for one—a few years ago, when architect Paul Bierman-Lytle and I were collaborating on a book about ecological building. Paul was just unveiling his design for a house nestled into a mountainside in a canyon near Sun Valley, Idaho.

In the 1920s, Le Corbusier declared that a house "is a machine to live in." What he meant was that a dwelling should be not only attractive but also efficient, like all those machines that were revolutionizing industry at the time. Paul's house for the Sawtooth foothills turns Le Corbusier's statement on its head: like a handful of other structures on the cutting edge of ecological design, it's a living machine, a dwelling suffused with wild habitats that double as human life-support systems.

The last I heard, work on the house had been suspended because the owner was in poor health. But imagine, as I often do, that construction has been completed: from a distance, the house is barely discernible from the surrounding terrain, only a glimmer of sunlight reflected from its crystalline shapes giving it away. The natural house, Wright wrote, should grow from its site, out of the ground and into the light, "as dignified as a tree in the midst of nature." The Idaho home rises naturally from its mountain aerie, anchored by a base of native stone, its peaked glass rooflines, like flawlessly polished metamorphic rock, reaching toward the sky.

Entering the house is like entering a forest. To either side of the sculpted glass doors are the living spaces. Straight ahead is the canopy of an indoor forest, a riparian ecosystem comprising a variety of terrestrial, wetland, and aquatic habitats. It is reached by a staircase that winds down to the forest floor, much like a canyon walk.

Water, forest, earth, and sky are all part of the living environment. A snow-fed stream on the site flows through the greenhouse; the water is pumped up and into the living room, where it cascades down rocks like a miniature waterfall, providing soothing sounds and humidifying the air with spray. Transparent bedroom roofs offer uninterrupted views of the nighttime sky; as they drift off to sleep, the inhabitants can gaze into deep space, light-years away. By day, window walls throughout the living spaces frame earthly mountain vistas.

The indoor wetlands and forest, however, are where the house truly breaks with tradition and ushers in a new era of architecture. The riparian habitat isn't just another living space boasting some unique features; it's a living ecosystem. Human shelter thus merges with wild habitat.

The indoor ecosystem adds beauty to the indoor environment and repairs the ruptured link between nature and daily life—even in this high-elevation climate, in which winter temperatures regularly plunge below zero. Just as important, it mitigates the adverse impacts of human activity on the site. It cleanses the air of indoor pollutants while creating oxygen and adding humidity.

Another set of indoor ecosystems purifies all the water used in the home. In an attached greenhouse, a Living Technology system developed by biologist John Todd cleanses polluted water, including sewage, in a series of sun-bathed translucent cylinders. Each is a functioning aquatic ecosystem, complete with algae, bacteria, snails, and higher plants, which feed on the waste. From here the water moves into small, man-made marshes where even more pollutants are extracted. The Living Technology system also allows the water to be diverted for other uses or further treatments—for example, it can flow into the riparian ecosystem to support its plants and fish, or be piped to the toilets and used for flushing. At the Idaho house, no contaminated water leaves the site; all water is purified in indoor ecosystems and then recycled, so it is used two or three times or even more.

Herbs, salad greens, and selected vegetables grow in a bioshelter off the kitchen. Additional fruits and nuts are grown in the interior forest, as well as outdoors, in a high-desert garden.

Ecologically viable habitat for the human species depends on a diversity of plant and animal species, as this twenty-first century home attests. Nature permeates the structure. In return, the indoor ecosystems support human life.

The Wild Garden

As early as 1625, Francis Bacon asserted that the ideal garden should include a "heath or wilderness." It was one of the first recorded calls for a more natural landscape. The gardens of Bacon's day were highly formal spreads with knotted hedges and perfect symmetry; he described his new ideal, by contrast, as "nature imitated and tactfully adorned."

"Nature tactfully adorned"—invoking images of statuesque trees on a sweep of green lawn—is as good a description as any of the typical late-twentieth-century North American garden. This kind of manicured woodland may have been state-of-the-art landscaping in the seventeenth century, but it is nature much *too* tactfully adorned for an age whose natural verdure is being stripped bare.

For decades, perhaps centuries, gardeners have played a largely unrecognized role in the preservation of some species— *Franklinia alatamaha,* for instance. This spectacular small tree, which offers white blooms in late summer and round, nutlike fruits that cling to the branches after the leaves fall, was collected along the banks of the Altamaha River in Georgia in 1770 by botanist John Bartram. Just twenty years later, *Franklinia* could no longer be found in the wild, but thanks to Bartram's efforts, the species survives today in gardens up and down the East Coast.

These days, a more comprehensive approach to preservation is necessary. The fifty years of intensive development since the end of World War II and the birth of suburbia have reduced the natural landscape to patches and fragments that in many areas are few and far between. And so the new ecological garden goes to great lengths to preserve not just individual species, but also entire habitats. In relatively undeveloped areas, the floor plans of new homes may be pushed and pulled to save a tree or rocky outcrop or arroyo. Les and Susan Wallach's house in the Sonoran Desert outside Tucson, for example, began with aerial photos and topographic and hydrological surveys. These studies suggested that the northern end of the property was the most suitable place to locate the structure: it offered the highest elevation for picturesque views of the city and the distant Santa Rita and Tucson Mountains, and the saguaros were spaced far enough apart to leave room for the footprint of a house. The floor plan evolved around an arroyo, or conduit for runoff from violent summer storms, that naturally bisects the site. Here and there the arroyo is studded with boulders that torrents of water have exposed over the centuries. The densest and most diverse native vegetation grows astride just such desert washes. Les, an architect, designed an enclosed "bridge" that spans the arroyo to connect the bedrooms with the public areas—the entrance, living room, and kitchen—located on the street side of the house. The actual construction aimed at conservation, too: to spare the desert flora, the foundation was laid one small section at a time, so that no additional land needed to be cleared for large stockpiles of mate-

Sonoran Desert natives saguaro
(Carnegiea gigantea) *and beard-tongue*
(Penstemon ambiguus).

rials. To further minimize the damage, the house was built from both sides of the arroyo, with no construction equipment being permitted to breach the fragile chasm.

At an 850-acre residential community across the state, in North Scottsdale, great care is being taken to protect another prime example of ruggedly beautiful Sonoran Desert etched with ravines and washes, dramatic rock outcroppings, fields of boulders, and a vast palette of indigenous plants, including majestic saguaros, squiggly, multistemmed ocotillos, barrel cacti, and other sculptural desert species, as well as softer palo verdes and desert willows and colorful wildflowers such as verbenas and penstemons. Throughout the development, called Desert Highlands, each building lot is surveyed and divided into three zones. The first, called the private area, comprises the actual footprint of the house and driveway. A buffer zone, or transitional area of ten to twenty-five feet, accommodates workers and equipment during the construction phase. All plants in these two areas are carefully dug up, boxed, and moved out of harm's way. Even the soil in these zones, full of nutrients and seeds native to the site, is dug up and temporarily set aside.

The third zone, called the natural area, which includes the most ecologically important topographic features, such as washes and undisturbed native flora, is absolutely sacrosanct. It is fenced off from the other areas during construction and protected in perpetuity. When construction is complete, the salvaged soil and plants are restored to the transitional area. Here, homeowners are free to add any drought-tolerant nonindigenous plants that don't distract aesthetically from the natural landscape. In the private spaces—courtyards, patios, and poolsides—they can grow thirsty tropicals as well. This careful approach to building can be applied anywhere, but it is particularly critical in areas where native habitats are vulnerable. Desert Highlands developer Gage Davis, an architect, landscape architect, and urban planner, says that though it may add about 5 percent to overall construction costs, that premium is more than offset by the savings incurred by not having to import a landscape, soil and plants, from scratch.

Fortunately, we're learning not only how to *avoid* doing ecological damage in the first place, but also how to *undo* it once it's been done. In areas where the natural landscape has been decimated—which in the United States is virtually everywhere—native plant communities are now being restored.

In the southern Appalachians, for example, gardeners are striving to re-create the densely layered woodlands in which North America's deciduous forest achieves its richest and most varied growth. Towering canopies of tulip tree, maple, buckeye, beech, and oak arch over understory species such as sorrel tree, with its drooping sprays of white summer flowers and its brilliant red-purple foliage in fall, and redbud, with its heart-shaped leaves and clusters of diminutive rosy-pink flowers in April. Showy shrubs such as *Rhododendron canescens*, an exquisite wild azalea that puts forth masses of fragrant white flowers, provide a procession of color from early April to mid-November. The rare and beautiful oconee bells and other woodland flowers burst into bloom in spring, followed by lush ferns, adding a fourth layer to the woodland community. Mosses blanket the forest floor. This layered effect may reach its pinnacle in the southern Appalachians, but it is typical throughout the eastern deciduous forest.

In my own Brooklyn backyard, where I'm replicating a tiny patch of the primeval oak forest that Henry Hudson and his crew found when they landed here, I've planted understory species such as shadbush under a canopy formed by tall trees in neighboring yards. The graceful silver-gray branches of this small tree ascend to a fan-shaped clump, and evanescent white flowers appear in spring, just as its downy new leaves begin to unfold. My shadbush and other native shrubs such as sweet pepperbush and New Jersey tea, which produce copious summer flowers to which bees and other pollinators flock, have created a charming setting for the spectacular cinnamon fern, the nodding yellow bellwort, and other wildflowers and ferns on my woodland garden's floor.

At a home on Mount Desert Island, landscape architect Patrick Chassé has restored a small portion of Maine's striking boreal forest. A circular driveway had severed the house—which sits on a coastal ledge at the tip of the only true fjord in the continental United States—from the surrounding spruce-fir forest. Pat knitted the house and forest back together using artfully placed stones (matched carefully in size, shape, and color to existing rocks on the site) and "native sod," a combination of native bunchberry, wintergreen, and haircap moss rescued from a blueberry farm. Now the owners stroll from the parking area to the house down a handsome path strewn with pine needles. Nearby, a natural rock outcropping became a focal point after Pat peeled away extraneous vegetation; water trickles down the exposed granite and plunges into a small pool below. Throughout the site, deft native plantings reproduce the generous massing, colors, and textures of plant associations in the wild. One secluded clearing is edged with a lush herbaceous border, where drifts of blue-gray foliage pick up the silvery tones of the boreal forest.

Gardeners in the Midwest are meanwhile re-creating native prairie on fifty-by-two-hundred-foot lots as well as on two-hundred-acre rural estates. On a five-acre site in Lake Forest, Illinois, landscape designer P. Clifford Miller had to contend with a large, wet prairie area that was being overrun by woody plants. Cliff restored the grassland community and put in a pond where the vegetation was too degraded to recover. Today, marsh phlox and Michigan lily tumble onto the long wooden walkway that connects the pond with the cedar deck of a handsome wood-and-stone prairie home. Somewhat drier areas were planted with such tallgrass-prairie denizens as prairie dock and pale purple coneflower. On a gentle knoll built up with spoils from the pond area, Cliff nurtured into being a bur oak savanna, one of this continent's most endangered habitats. This planting helps screen the house from the road. Behind the house, existing stands of aspen, a tree that colonizes the upland edges of wet prairie areas, were left to buffer the structure from adjacent properties. Cliff removed the nonnative species growing underneath the aspens and is now coaxing prairie wildflowers to move in around the edges.

Another wild garden outside Sun Valley, Idaho, links a striking solar home with the surrounding sagebrush steppe. Designed by landscape architect Bob Murase, it incorporates native flora almost universally ignored by Sun Valley residents: the ubiquitous sagebrush, a dozen native grasses, and wildflowers commonly found along ravines. A series of formal terrace gardens lined with stands of quaking aspen tumbles like a riverbed down the south side of the house. These elegant outdoor terraces terminate in a group of carefully arranged boulders brought in from a neighboring farm, which echo outcroppings on nearby hills. Native and naturalized species as well as a few cultivars were planted intensively among the boulders and around two paths that encircle the house, with sprays of shrubby cinquefoil interlaced with prairie flax and wild geranium. Beyond, wilder patches of grass and wild white yarrow blend freely into the scrubby vegetation of the Sawtooth foothills.

What these diverse natural gardens have in common is this: all are designed to enhance the sense of place, to meld easily with the surrounding native vegetation, and to restore what once flourished but has since been lost. Culturally, the wild garden alludes to the native landscapes that greeted the pioneers and that have for centuries imbued America with its sense of limitless possibility; biologically, it provides a sanctuary for beleaguered native species.

The ecological role played by gardeners is destined to become even more crucial in the future. While wildernesses in

North America continue to shrink, compromising the biological diversity of the planet, garden acreage is increasing. If the widely predicted global warming does occur (many scientists believe it has already begun), this acreage will become critical as the natural ranges of many plants shift radically and rapidly northward. Scientists and gardeners may have to help those species that are unable to migrate quickly enough to keep pace with changing conditions, by nurturing healthy populations in backyards as well as on public lands throughout the northern reaches of their ranges.

Wild gardens' potential as ecological sanctuaries is just beginning to be explored. In professional journals, conservation biologists, who specialize in the preservation of native species and habitats, have started to float proposals for a system of ecological reserves in bioregions around the world. Each bioregion would include a core area with minimal human activity (such as a Yellowstone or Yosemite in the American West), ringed by areas whose level of development would increase roughly in relation to their distance from the undisturbed core. The transitional areas might be subject to ecologically sensitive activities such as selective timber harvesting or well-thought-out housing development.

In such a system of practical landscape ecology, homeowners in transitional areas would be discouraged from tampering to any great extent with the native vegetation on their property. In most of the eastern United States, where no large undisturbed ecosystems remain, the few surviving natural fragments would need to be preserved and the surrounding areas restored so that eventually there would be sizable, self-sustaining tracts of natural landscape. Because suburban backyards blanket the East Coast from Boston to Richmond and beyond, home gardeners would obviously play a major role in the restoration effort. Someday, perhaps, these wild gardens may be linked to form a network of corridors crisscrossing the continent, connecting the bigger nature reserves to allow animals to move freely and plant seeds to disperse. Even tiny wild gardens like mine in the middle of the city, unable to connect with large tracts of natural landscape, can link us metaphorically with the rest of nature by representing sacred ground, serving as an homage to the biota that preceded us.

The wild garden is the spiritual core of the modern landscape, a Western version of the Zen dry garden epitomized by the garden of the Buddhist sanctuary of Ryoan-ji. Created near Kyoto, Japan, around 1480, that garden encompasses a rectangular area covered with fine gravel raked in strictly defined, wavy patterns. There are no trees, no shrubs, no flowers—just fifteen stones arranged in groups of five, two, three, two, and three, in such a way that regardless of where you stand, at least one stone is always visible. The moss on these irregularly shaped rocks is the only trace of time, or of passage of any kind. The garden is to be contemplated in the quest for enlightenment, that pure intuition of the nature of things as an organic whole (including the people who contemplate the landscape) which is at the core of the Zen philosophy of life.

The sand in the Ryoan-ji garden represents the universe, a void in which float the rocks, material objects existing in time. The human mind is a similar void, into which float thoughts occasioned by worldly events. This is the necessary unity of mind and matter that the Ryoan-ji garden is designed to help us perceive.

Likewise, though in a more typically activist Western fashion, the wild garden is concerned with our relationship with the universal life force, which we know as evolution. In the wild garden, human habitat merges with the ancient native landscape, and the link between nature and daily life is restored. We interact with nature on a day-to-day basis, not just on two-week jaunts to some far-off national park. This perception of the wild garden as harmonizing with the cultivated garden, of course, also implies the opposite, suggesting that the cultivated garden is capable of being perceived as a natural extension of the native landscape, not just a corruption of it.

In the wild garden, we embrace ourselves as a species, not simply as separate individuals, families, or factions. Above all else, the wild garden is a place where we embrace not only human desires and visions of meaning and significance, but also the longings and visions of the other kingdoms and other life forms with which we share this world.

The Front Garden

"Suburbs," Erma Bombeck once wrote, "are small, controlled communities where for the most part everyone has the same living standards, the same number of garbage cans, the same house plans, and the same level in the septic tanks." And, she might have added, the same front yards.

I first gave the matter some serious thought after hearing a lecture by C. Colston Burrell. For months Cole, one of the most talented garden designers I know, had been studying the question of why virtually every suburban landscape in North America consists of emerald turf from lot line to lot line, a large shade tree off the corner of the house, and a collection of sculpted or, worse, scalped shrubs lined up against the foundation. As part of his master's research at the University of Minnesota's Department of Landscape Architecture, he was trying to figure out how to get suburbanites to budge, even a little, from this formula. In the backyard, some Americans may dare to be different, but the front yard remains the province of respectability and the horticulturally hidebound.

Any suburban homeowner can attest to the fact that one of a garden's most important functions is to demonstrate solidarity with one's neighbors. In contemporary America, that means having a manicured lawn: the average American would rather live next to a white-collar criminal than next to someone with a weedy yard. At least 75 percent of the typical front garden is given over to turf.

Another indication of neighborliness is an unobstructed view from the sidewalk or street to the front entrance of the house. We make no bones about how to get to our doorsteps. Foundation plantings also help to direct visitors by framing the front door. The passion for shrubs set against the base of the house began during Victorian times, when bushes made the big homes of the era seem more grounded to their sites. The custom persisted, however, even as houses and building lots shrank. Today, shrubs planted along the foundation can quickly dwarf a small house. To keep junipers, forsythias, and arborvitae from totally blocking paths and windows, drastic pruning is necessary. The shearing of front-garden shrubs has in turn created a kind of staccato pattern across the facade of the typical house, with the vertical evergreens flanking the front door followed by horizontal lines of clipped shrubs under the front windows, leading to another set of vertical exclamation points at the house's corners.

The front yard has other inviolate elements as well. A shade tree placed strategically off the corner of the house or in the middle of the lawn is essential, and houses in more urbanized areas will have at least a street tree or two. A few flowers complete the picture. Lined up in front of the foundation shrubs or planted in a circle around a shade tree or lamppost, they add a dollop of seasonal color and, like a well-tended lawn, indicate that the owners take pride in their property and their neighborhood.

Lately, privacy screens, whether fences or hedges, have crept into the equation, too, though at one time they were considered a sign of poor breeding. Andrew Jackson Downing, author of the influential *Treatise on the Theory and Practice of Landscape Gardening* (1841) and one of North America's original horticultural gurus, deemed fences "unsightly" and "offensive." "Nothing is

The traditional American front garden.

more common, in the places of cockneys who become inhabitants of the country," he wrote, "than a display immediately
around the dwelling of a spruce paling of carpentry, neatly made,
and painted white or green; an abomination among the fresh
fields, of which no person of taste could be guilty." Horticulturist
Frank J. Scott, whose book *The Art of Beautifying Suburban Home
Grounds* was the bible for late-Victorian homeowners, didn't
have much use for hedges, either: "One of the barbarisms of old
gardening," he called them, "as absurd and unchristian in our day
as the walled courts and barred windows of a Spanish cloister."

Downing and Scott did more than anybody else to codify
the national front-yard aesthetic, eclipsing a variety of regional
traditions. In New England, for example, enclosed dooryard
gardens in the cottage-garden style once provided herbs and
vegetables for daily use, as well as flowers for pleasure. In the
Southwest and in Florida, the Spanish influence resulted in
courtyards that were at least partially enclosed by adobe or
stucco walls, creating private entrances as well as outdoor rooms.
In the old neighborhoods of Charleston and New Orleans,
entrances were located on the side of the house, with access via
side gardens entered through a gate along the sidewalk. These
enclosed, self-contained gardens were largely abandoned in the
last half of the nineteenth century, when the English landscape
style captured the popular imagination.

Downing modified the English landscape garden, which had
originally been created for the country houses of the English gentry, to suit the tastes of upper- and upper-middle-class American
suburbanites. Born in Newburgh, New York, in 1815, he inherited a nursery from his father but soon moved into the more
lucrative field of landscape design. His *Treatise* was revised several times and went through sixteen printings before 1879.
Despite his humble beginnings, the failure of his nursery, and a
bankruptcy from which he was saved only by the largesse of his
friends, Downing was a snob. He divided domestic architecture

into three "classes": the modest cottage; the farmhouse, a larger but still utilitarian structure; and the villa, a substantial dwelling that required the care of at least a handful of servants. This last "class" was the ideal, of course, and Downing likewise believed that only spacious grounds of hundreds of acres would allow humans to live in harmony with nature. However, he did deign to note that even the owner of a small cottage could make its grounds "tasteful" and "agreeable" by "attempting only the simple and natural." By "simple and natural" he meant a landscape pared down to a few essentials: "a soft, verdant lawn, a few forest or ornamental trees well grouped, walks, and a few flowers."

In the typical Downing landscape, a veil of trees added intrigue to the drive up to the house and could also be used to improve the lines of a less-than-perfect structure. Trees, he wrote, "are like the drapery which covers a somewhat ungainly figure, and while it conceals its defects, communicates to it new interest and expression." Of utmost importance, though, was a finely undulating lawn, both to unify the composition and, in the front of the house, to afford a clear view to the door.

At around this same time, lawn was also being championed by Frederick Law Olmsted, who designed a number of suburbs as well as parks. Olmsted believed that the front lawn of a house in the suburbs pulled together the entire residential composition and lent it not only an air of openness and freedom but also a sense of community.

The American front yard thus became part of the glue that holds this society together. But it is tearing apart the larger fabric of plant and animal life.

Although a flawless front lawn in a tidy front yard may imply an owner who is courteous and social, it is beginning to take on negative connotations, too. The pesticides and herbicides routinely applied to such lawns pose health risks for people and animals. Fertilizing leads to nutrient overloading in lakes and streams, and irrigation reduces already limited water supplies.

The vertical and horizontal structures of native plant communities are entirely fragmented in the suburban front yard. In any healthy woodland, there are a number of vertical layers of vegetation, from the tree canopy down to the wildflowers and ferns on the forest floor; in healthy grasslands, the gamut runs from the tallest forbs and grasses to the smallest violets. The more layers, the more diverse the vegetation, and the more feeding and nesting opportunities for wildlife. In the average front yard, there's a tree canopy in the middle of the lawn or along the street, a shrub layer along the house, and never the twain shall meet. To make matters worse, the diversity of the ground layer—that is, the lawn—has been drastically reduced. Even lawns that are grown organically and allowed to brown out during droughts fail to address a fundamental ecological problem: these monocultures are the horticultural equivalent of ethnic cleansing, a denial of the fact that plants are members of diverse natural communities.

Suburbia's turf matrix does not work as a bridge between fragmented islands of wild habitat. It prevents many animals from moving and seeds from dispersing. The result is a landscape devoid of biodiversity.

A GROWING BODY of research suggests that the American view of naturalness and nature is trapped in an aesthetic time warp. This research leaves no doubt that people prefer landscapes that are natural; the problem is our perception of exactly what "natural" means.

The naturalness that Americans admire today has much more to do with eighteenth-century notions of the picturesque and beautiful—that is, well-spaced canopy trees on a neat, rolling expanse of turf—than with what modern scientists have discovered about the way nature works. This cultural obsolescence makes us prefer some kinds of vegetation over others: for example, one study of owners of rare ecoystems in Minnesota found that oak woodlands are appreciated much more than either wetlands or prairies. And even when it comes to woodland, it seems it is possible to have too much of a good thing: the understory of dense woodlands is often cleared of shrubs and dead wood. According to Joan Nassauer, a professor of landscape architecture at the University of Minnesota, it is difficult to introduce biodiversity into the suburban landscape because our cultural concept of "picturesque" nature causes us to favor landscapes that look tended, which we perceive to be the opposite of wild. A prairie or a meadow or a woodland with a rich understory, even one painstakingly re-created in a residential setting, tends to be interpreted as messy, exhibiting a lack of care.

A few years ago, Nassauer conducted an interesting experiment. She asked more than two hundred Minnesotans to rate seven different landscapes in their order of preference. One was the conventional lawn with a few ornamental plants; the second was the same layout but with a weedy, unkempt lawn. Most of the others featured some of the familiar elements of the suburban front yard, but each bent the rules to a varying degree, aiming for a more biodiverse landscape through the addition of indigenous plants and structural complexity.

The first variation (treatment three) retained a mowed lawn, but native canopy trees such as oak, cedar, and aspen took the place of more traditional ornamental varieties. In the next (treatment four), 50 percent of the mowed turf was replaced by a prairie plant mix heavily dominated by flowers. In treatment five, the prairie mix was substituted for 75 percent of the lawn. In another variation (treatment six), 50 percent of the lawn yielded to indigenous sumac and hazelnut shrubs. The final landscape (treatment seven) had by far the greatest diversity of plant species, the most structural complexity, and the largest area of viable wildlife habitat: 75 percent of the turf was replaced by a combination of indigenous shrubs and canopy trees, with prairie wildflowers growing along the edges.

Nassauer's recruits pronounced the treatment with the most minor ecological improvement—the mowed turf and native tree canopy (number three)—attractive, well cared for, and very neat. They felt that though the design in which 50 percent of the lawn was converted to a floriferous prairie was not as neat as either the first landscape or the third treatment, it was just as, or even slightly more, attractive, and distinctly more natural. After that, the correlation of attractiveness with ecological complexity began to break down because of a perceived lack of care—in other words, the higher ecological quality represented by the fifth, sixth, and seventh treatments appeared to violate the conventional view of the tidy suburban landscape. These designs were seen as uncared for and much too messy. The seventh treatment, the most ecologically complete plant community, was judged to be very messy and unattractive, though not quite as bad as the weedy lawn (number two).

Thirty years' worth of evidence on the health and environmental risks of pesticides has begun to put a dent in the chemical lawn-care industry, as many homeowners now think twice before using toxic pesticides in their yards. But how to get suburbanites to take the next big step toward a more ecological landscape, to move beyond the picturesque and learn to value biodiversity? This is the issue that makes the landscape intellectual's blood boil these days. For the last ten years, Joan Nassauer and other academics concerned about the dearth of biological diversity in ever-expanding suburbia have been debating how best to advance a revolution in the landscape as complete as the one begun by Downing more than 150 years ago.

In traditional academic fashion, the debate pits the highbrows against the lowbrows. The highbrows believe that Art created by great garden designers and earthwork artists will lead the way to a new ecological landscape aesthetic. Art, in their view, has an uncanny ability to anticipate society, and the new environmental artists will help reveal to the rest of us the ecological patterns that underlie life's surfaces. The lowbrows are skeptical about any approach that depends on either a utopian or an elitist conception of art.

Joan Nassauer is definitely in the latter camp. She believes in going right to the heart of the problem: the conventional suburban landscape itself. In her view, the best way to make a biodiverse garden more appealing to the typical suburbanite is to portray or "frame" it with more familiar landscape elements. In the suburbs, that means incorporating landscaping cues that denote care. The aesthetic of stewardship—or the propensity of people to display themselves as caretakers of nature—is, she points out, a human trait that cuts across cultural lines. Other ethnic groups may not express their care for the landscape in precisely the same way that we do in the North American suburbs, but the impulse is substantially consistent. The Acoma people in New Mexico who engage in dryland farming, for example, express their care through an intricate pattern of gourd vines intercropped with corn planted in mounds. No matter what the culture, argues Nassauer, the way to protect and promote healthy ecological systems is "by putting our human stamp upon them, by clearly showing our intention for them to exist."

Cole Burrell, a student of Nassauer's, has been able to design many ecologically sensitive gardens that his urban and suburban clients can happily live with. Neatnik gardeners, he says, need only to be reassured that a biodiverse landscape won't garner tickets from the weed police or nasty notes from the neighbors. Cole's gardens take considerable license with those inviolate elements of the front yard that are most resistant to change. Lawn, for example, is invariably reduced, often to a minimum of a few mowing strips, just to let everyone know that the yard is cared for and that it indeed looks the way it is intended to—by design, not through neglect. In Cole's words, "Mown strips along the street and adjacent property lines create an orderly frame. Within the frame, you are free to innovate with exuberant perennial gardens, a meadow or prairie, even a small woodland—depending on the look you want and your region of the country." Cole also integrates foundation plantings with trees and flowers. Sometimes the shrubs are replaced entirely by herbaceous plantings; other times, shade trees are clustered together and a full woodland understory is added. He excises typically skimpy rows of annual flowers and puts in more extensive plantings of annuals and perennials and often grasses, or else adds the flowers to shrub or woodland plantings.

While many of Cole's gardens include only regionally native plants, others do not. His own garden is an example: an obsessive plant collector, Cole has found it impossible to limit his plant palette to local natives, even in central Minnesota, his current home, where woodland, prairie, and oak savanna meet in a kind of ecological crossroads, and where natural plant diversity is accordingly high. The oak savanna, a parklike plant community of prairie plants punctuated by spreading bur oaks with shade-tolerant species growing underneath, did, however, serve as the inspiration for the landscape design of his 60-by-150-foot lot. The space is dominated by a huge, spreading, multistemmed box elder; he used this and the other trees on the lot as the canopy structure and connected them to the horizontal ground plane with shrubs and herbaceous plants. Woodland plants grow in the shade of the trees, while the open areas constitute the "prairie." Still, Cole's garden is quite formal in its layout.

In keeping with traditional front-yard norms of neighborliness, the walk up to the door is unobstructed, framed by two strips of mowed lawn. To the right of the walk is a dry shade garden under a hackberry tree, featuring drought-tolerant savanna plants such as starry Solomon's plume, sedges, and interrupted fern. To the left is a series of exuberant, prairielike herbaceous borders eight feet deep, enclosing a small square of lawn on three sides. In early spring, the lawn area can be seen from the street, and a profusion of spring bulbs and perennials enjoyed from both inside and out. The color scheme features purple, blue, and white flowers in early summer, with pale yellow used sparingly as an accent. In midsummer, when I saw it, yellows predominated. Stately silphiums and coreopsis, as well as prairie smoke, mountain mint, and a dazzling multitude of other perennials, were all in full bloom, and the tall prairie plants completely enveloped the lawn, making it a quiet retreat. Late summer and autumn bring asters, goldenrods, gentians, and grasses. In winter, the golden and russet stalks provide visual interest, as well as food and cover for wildlife.

The fourth side of the small square of lawn in the front yard, the side along the house, is a wetland border that Cole created by excavating an eight-by-twenty-five-foot trench, two feet deep, which he then lined with plastic and filled with rich compost. This bog, filled with water-loving plants such as native turtleheads, monkey flower, and vervain, along with nonindigenous ligularias, rodgersias, and primroses, is "watered" by the runoff from the roof and requires no supplemental irrigation.

At a time when Americans are seeming more divided by the day, the front yard's traditional statement of shared community values should definitely be applauded. With its mowed strips of lawn and its formal layout, Cole's garden is neat enough to satisfy the neighbors. However, as the human population grows and wild lands and wild creatures disappear, it's essential that we strive to demonstrate solidarity with the larger ecological community as well. Scores of plant species grow in the front and back yards of Cole's quarter-acre lot. The diversity of birds (one hundred twenty species), butterflies (fourteen species), bees, and other insects and animals (four species) that feed, take refuge, and nest there offer ample proof that the design is working ecologically, too.

The Kitchen Garden

In the foyer of my parents' house is the family photo gallery. There are portraits of stern Italian ancestors, and a snapshot of my dad as a dashing adolescent in knickers—with a full head of hair! There's a hand-colored photo of my mom when she graduated from high school, the mortarboard crowning her radiant, as-yet-unlined face. There's also a picture of my grandma, my mother's mother, digging in the garden, dressed in the uniform of any self-respecting Italian grandmother of her day: a black dress, with a kerchief tied around her head.

Grandma and I weren't the best of friends. One of the low points of my young life was the day she moved in with us, when I had to give up my spacious second-floor bedroom for a claustrophobic little room downstairs. Grandma could be severe and unforgiving, and my budding feminist soul revolted every time she tsked that I should be washing the dishes as she let my brother run off with his friends. (I steadfastly refused, of course, and as my husband, Don, will tell you, I've washed precious few ever since.)

It's only lately, years after her death, that I've come to realize how much I learned from her. In fact, some of my fondest childhood memories are of Grandma and the garden: Grandma sticking puny twigs in the ground that later became strapping fig trees loaded with luscious fruits; Grandma spreading out on a table the seeds from the summer's biggest, juiciest tomatoes so they could dry and be sowed as next year's crop; Grandma hanging tin pie plates on our two cherry trees to scare away the birds—much to my mother's chagrin. In the postwar suburbs where we lived, a well-manicured yard was much appreciated, but a useful tree, shrub, or herb—much less one with tin plates hanging off of it— was definitely déclassé. It was, and pretty much still is, a sign of status in the suburbs to plant only purely ornamental plants.

In the 1960s, when I was growing up, the Green Revolution was in full swing. These were the go-go years of modern agriculture, when farmers and gardeners were using massive doses of petrochemical fertilizers, pesticides, herbicides, and fungicides without giving it a second thought. Rototillers, riding mowers, and weed whackers, as well as tractors, combines, and the like, all powered by petroleum, were replacing horses and human muscle power. New varieties of plants scarcely capable of fending for themselves without petrochemicals and the internal combustion engine were becoming the norm. Vast acreages of seed annuals suited to mass-production techniques were wiping out traditional agricultural ecosystems.

The result has been unprecedented yield. The new breeds of corn, wheat, and rice that gave the Green Revolution its name have helped eliminate famine in many parts of the world. Only inveterate optimists, however, believe that modern industrial agriculture can be sustained over the long haul. The tradeoff for high yields has been polluted streams, poisoned water, and a destabilizing dependence on Middle Eastern oil. Tillage has also taken its toll: the constant disturbance has reduced the microbial activity that revitalizes the soil; deteriorated the structure of the soil and thereby inhibited its ability to hold minerals and water; and, by exposing the soil for long periods, made it vulnerable to erosion by wind and water.

Crop diversity has been yet another casualty. Modern cultivars of food crops possess traits that have been fixed and maintained through the mass selection of those few plants that have certain desirable characteristics. Increasingly, the choices available to farmers and backyard growers are F_1 hybrids, which are the product of the first generation of crosses between two pure lines. This virtually guarantees that the plants you buy will have the desirable traits—such as resistance to verticillium wilt in a tomato—and also that the breeders will be sure to get your business again next year, because if you plant the seeds of an F_1 hybrid, you won't be assured of a disease-resistant plant.

For hundreds of years, humans played a major role in diversifying the gene pools of crops. Wherever we went, we carried the major food species with us; and wherever we took them, they were modified both by the new environment and by the methods we used to grow them. In this way, hundreds of locally adapted varieties of the same crop, called landraces, evolved.

Domestication led not only to the evolution of new variations but also to a proliferation of new forms. Thus, for example, from the single species *Brassica oleracea*, a wild cabbage native to coastal western and southern Europe, we got not only a multitude of cultivated cabbages but also kale, cauliflower, collards, broccoli, kohlrabi, and brussels sprouts.

Purebred cultivars began to replace landraces in Europe in the mid-1800s; a mere fifty years later, few if any of the major landrace crops remained on the continent. Selection of cultivars from landraces was largely superseded in the twentieth century by crossbreeding in all major crops. Today, even many of the earliest cultivars no longer survive. And so we're left with a few near-pure lines, hybrids, and clones of crops such as onions and potatoes that are propagated vegetatively. To make matters worse, the wild forebears of some crops are now extinct—for example, the faba bean, *Vicia faba*.

The same new crop-breeding techniques that have brought astonishing improvements in productivity have also resulted in a high degree of genetic uniformity. This trend "has placed in jeopardy the reservoirs of genetic diversity on which the continuing evolution of cultivated plants to a large degree depends," according to *The Conservation of Plant Biodiversity*, a recent work by three Australian researchers, published by Cambridge University Press.

The genetic vulnerability of advanced crop cultivars became

Wild cabbage (Brassica oleracea),
top left, and a few of its cultivated forms. Clockwise from top right:
cabbage, kale, Brussels sprouts, cauliflower, kohlrabi;
center, broccoli.

a widespread concern in 1970, when an epidemic of southern corn-leaf blight destroyed about 15 percent of the corn crop in the United States. There were two major reasons for this: first, the corn crop uniformly lacked the genes that confer resistance to leaf blight, and second, the same susceptible variety was used over a vast area. This kind of vulnerability is becoming an all-too-frequent phenomenon in many crops as their genetic base narrows. In rice, for instance, there has been a drastic reduction of genetic diversity due both to the decision on the part of breeders in several different countries to employ the same gene to produce short plants, and to the extensive use of cytoplasm derived from China in the breeding of semidwarf cultivars.

As wild species are husbanded by humans over many generations, they undergo a series of predictable changes in their genetic makeup, which scientists call the "domestication syndrome." They become easier to grow, and produce the desired product more reliably and abundantly, whether it be the seeds of cereals or the tubers of potatoes. The valuable (to us) parts of the plant—that is, seed, fruit, root, stem, tuber—grow huge; scientists call this phenomenon gigantism. The plant then has to change its growth form to support the giant part or parts. We also tamper with the plants' sex life. Sexual reproduction in some crops is suppressed, to the benefit of those edible parts— for example, the tubers of potatoes—that are produced vegetatively. The plants' dispersal methods are likewise constrained: seeds are retained longer in the fruit or inflorescence, and in the case of potatoes, the length of the stolons, or shoots on which the tubers grow, decreases, making the crops much easier to harvest.

This is all well and good for us. However, the domesticated plants, unlike their wild ancestors, are often utterly dependent upon people for their growth and reproduction. And, too, for their evolution: in traditional agriculture, farmers and gardeners (like my grandmother) collected their own seeds. The plants reproduced sexually, and natural selection pressures could run their course. Plants and pests could slug it out over the generations, and only the fittest would survive. Grandma's biggest, juiciest tomato was not only the tastiest but also likely the best equipped genetically to deter the insects and diseases that were most rampant at the time. In modern agriculture, by contrast, seeds are bought, and plant breeding and commercial pressures result in genetically uniform cultivars. Even these cultivars are not allowed to evolve naturally: evolution is entirely in the hands of a few breeders, occurring only as they replace old cultivars with new ones.

The enormous blow struck to biodiversity by the loss of wild species, landraces, and early cultivars is a potential catastrophe. Plant breeders need these as potential gene donors, especially in breeding for resistance to diseases and pests. Moreover, because these varieties evolved or were bred before the advent of petrochemical fertilizers, intensive cultivation, and extensive irrigation, they could be crucial to the success of a new, ecological agriculture.

I LEARNED AT a tender young age not to overromanticize the life of the soil. When I was eight, I found myself locked in a contest of pride with my brother, George, to see which of us could have fifty square feet of the vegetable garden weeded, tilled, and planted first. I ran to the garage to get the cultivator and other hand tools. I toiled, I sweated, my hands became raw with blisters. George, four years older and much cleverer than me, teased me for what seemed like an eternity but was probably more like two or three hours. Then he borrowed the neighbor's rototiller. And promptly finished first.

Such traumas, I've found, cultivate a certain intellectual bent. At least that's my excuse for spending most of my life in front of a computer instead of on a farm. But despite my early setback, I still love growing vegetables. There's something fundamental about it.

Ask any kid these days where food comes from, and he or she will reply smartly, "The supermarket!" In my Brooklyn neighborhood, the answer would probably be the local takeout place. For decades, the only link to the age-old rhythms of agriculture for most of us has been the produce section of Waldbaum's or Winn Dixie. We've lost all sense of depending on the soil for our daily sustenance. The typical suburban yard, if it includes vegetables at all, banishes them to a spot behind the garage, the way old living-room furniture is moved unceremoniously to the basement to make way for trendier decor.

The kitchen garden allows us to complete the natural cycle of gardening and cooking. In our own backyards, we can grow plants that please the mouth as well as the eye, from the sculptural, lime-green 'Romanesco' broccoli to the magnificent Mediterranean herb lovage, with its distinctive flavor, like pungent celery with a hint of lemon and anise. We can grow rare heirloom varieties, and by so doing save them from extinction. We can have a bountiful harvest without pesticides or fertilizers made from fossil fuels.

Since the 1960s, a number of pioneers have developed advanced ecological techniques that build on ancient systems of peasant agriculture. They've paved the way for the creation of new ecological kitchen gardens that mimic native ecosystems by recycling nutrients to revitalize the soil, and by incorporating diverse communities of food crops best suited to their particular region.

One of these horticultural innovators was Robert Rodale. For many years he and his father, J. I. Rodale, were among the few advocates of agricultural alternatives in North America. Their Rodale Research Center has carried out extensive research on many aspects of ecological agriculture, though it's probably best known for formulating composting and soil-building techniques that can simulate natural nutrient cycles both on farms and in gardens.

Between the 1930s and the 1960s, Alan Chadwick developed the biodynamic/French intensive method of crop production. Although Chadwick, an Englishman, did not introduce his new method into the United States until the 1960s, at the four-acre organic student garden at the University of California, Santa Cruz, the method itself actually combined two older techniques dating back to turn-of-the-century and 1920s Europe. French intensive gardening, originally developed in the 1890s outside Paris, called for crops to be grown in eighteen inches of horse manure, a readily available fertilizer back then. The plants were packed so close together that they formed a microclimate and a living mulch that kept out weeds and prevented water from evaporating from the soil. Glass cloches were used in winter to extend the growing season, enabling gardeners to produced up to nine crops a year. The biodynamic technique was devised in the 1920s by the Austrian Rudolf Steiner, who attributed the decline in crop yields and the increase in insect and disease problems in Europe at the time to the use of synthetic fertilizers and pesticides. Among other things, he advocated the use of organic fertilizers and raised planting beds.

The garden that Chadwick and his apprentices took on at Santa Cruz was on the side of a hill, with a poor, clayey soil. Within two to three years they had nonetheless created a healthy, productive soil through the use of prodigious amounts of compost.

Chadwick's biodynamic/French intensive system employs raised beds twelve inches deep and three to six feet wide. Between the beds are narrow pathways for walking and for wheeling equipment. Each bed contains a rich mixture of native soil and either manure or compost, which, depending on the composition of the original soil, can constitute up to 75 percent of the mixture.

Chadwick's work has been further developed and popularized by California horticulturist John Jeavons. Jeavons's research has shown that in a six-month growing season, a backyard gardener, if so inclined, can grow a year's worth of fruits and vegetables (322 pounds) on one hundred square feet of earth, working an average of only five to ten minutes a day. In his book *How to Grow More Vegetables than You Ever Thought Possible on Less Land than You Can Imagine*, he writes, "The biointensive method appears to allow anyone to take 'the worst possible soil' (Alan Chadwick's appraisal of our research site) and turn it into a bountiful garden." After years of testing, his system has produced yields that are on average four to six times greater than those typical of American agriculture, even though his water and energy use is well below the norm for commercial agriculture. The next question to be answered is whether it is possible to produce all the fertilizer necessary on the site.

The new ecological kitchen garden aims to mimic not only the natural nutrient cycle but also the structures and interactions of plant communities native to the area. A community of species created by humans is known as a guild; ideally, each member of such a guild provides for some of the needs of at least one other member. The best-known guild in North America is the squash, beans, and maize combination first grown by many Indian tribes. As the cornstalks shoot upward, the bean vines wind around them and thus manage to move up into the sunlight, too. The leguminous beans help supply nutrients for the corn and squash by fixing nitrogen in the soil. The squash plants in turn spread over the ground at the base of the corn and bean plants, covering and protecting the soil and stymieing weeds. Once again, modern agriculture has replaced

such basic plant communities with monocultures, or vast plantings of a single crop, whose needs must be satisfied by infusions of
petrochemicals.

A handful of visionaries have gone beyond guilds to create
agroecological communities that much more closely imitate
native ecosystems. These new plant communities reflect the
structure of the local vegetation and are also designed for succession—that is, to grow and change continuously over time into
"climax" states that, like those of native plant communities,
are long-lived and represent the most complex and diverse
assemblages of living organisms possible for their particular environment and climate.

One of the most influential advocates of successional agriculture is Bill Mollison, who coined the term "permaculture" for his
integrated, evolving system of perennial or self-perpetuating
plant and animal species of use to humans. Permaculture mirrors
the natural process of succession, which over time creates ecosystems that are effective and stable utilizers of space, energy, and
living elements. Each year, smaller and smaller amounts of fertilizer and other inputs are needed.

For Mollison, who developed permaculture in Australia, the
climax state of ecological agriculture is a simulation of forest;
other gardeners whose native environments are grasslands,
deserts, and other biomes work with variations on those native
plant communities. In his book *Permaculture One*, Mollison
writes that permaculture, "unlike modern annual crop culture,
has the potential for continuous evolution towards a desirable
climax state. Annual crops are destroyed when harvested and
must be replanted, whereas in permaculture the plants and animals, often long lived, grow and change with the system." He
notes that his own permaculture reflects the vertical structure of
a natural forest: "The great variety of plant types from large, top-
storey trees to herbs, creates habitat and food diversity, allowing

a complex array of fauna." The diversity of species and their complex interactions create a system of checks and balances that can help prevent epidemic outbreaks of pests.

A permaculture also reflects the horizontal structure or microclimates of a natural landscape. Such microclimates allow for an even greater range of useful species, as different communities of plants suited to different conditions of light, moisture, drainage, and airflow are all incorporated into the agricultural design. Depending on the particular microclimates it contains and on its distance from the house, a permaculture may encompass annual vegetables and herbs, perennial vegetables, grains, herbs, fruit and nut trees, or even livestock.

Mollison writes that though the yields per unit of area for any one species in a permaculture are likely to be lower than they would be in a conventional monoculture, the sum of yields will be greater because a single-species system can never use all the available energy and nutrients on a plot of land. Like a native forest, a multilayer permaculture can exploit all available sunlight for photosynthesis, and different plants with different-shaped root systems can tap different water and nutrient sources.

It may sound as if ecological agriculture is possible only on two-acre homesteads off winding country roads, but an enormous amount of food can in fact be grown organically even in the inner city, provided that gardeners are willing to replace purely decorative plantings with crops. Community gardens are already flourishing in some urban areas. Even in small backyards, a shade tree can be replaced by a fruit or nut tree, and a sunlit wall can become a backdrop for espaliered fruit and vine crops. The Gaia Institute in New York has shown that a cornucopia of fresh fruits and vegetables can be produced on city rooftops.

In *Permaculture Two*, Mollison advises neophytes to "start at your doorstep," and that's just what Don and I have done in our little Brooklyn backyard. Of course, we had little choice because it's the only place where there's any sun. By our back door, on a four-by-eight-foot platform from which a circular staircase winds down to the yard, is our tiny kitchen garden. Everything grows in containers: spring and fall lettuce crops, as well as a variety of herbs, including parsley, basil, tarragon, and lovage. Pole beans twine around the railings. And we grow a bumper crop of tomatoes, some of which are trellised against the south-facing brick wall of the house. It isn't exactly a permaculture yet, but we're working on it.

Whether you garden in the city or in the country, as Mollison notes, it is now possible to design a garden that "take[s] advantage of some of the resources of the whole world, and to consider species from every country, so that the potential diversity of even temperate regions can be greatly enriched"—to the point where that diversity can almost rival the biodiversity of the tropics. Heck, from China alone we could get hundreds of cultivars of persimmon and jujube, representing hundreds of years' worth of natural and cultural selection. We can also incorporate genetic diversity in our gardens by planting a variety not only of hybrids (for improved disease resistance) but also of locally adapted heirloom varieties, now available from a small but growing number of mail-order suppliers.

If we adopt this approach, we will enable both the crops and our new agricultural plant communities to evolve to meet changing conditions, whether new pests or a warming climate. They will likewise be able to evolve in concert with the wild landscape. At the New Alchemy Institute in Falmouth, Massachusetts, researchers working in indoor food-producing gardens demonstrated the salutary effects of what they called "ecological islands"—clusters of plants and beneficial animals left untouched but protected in intensively cultivated areas. The beneficial organisms took refuge in these islands, ranging out to search for crop pests only to return to the relatively safe and stable ecosystems. A hedgerow serves much the same function on a farm.

Even in the kitchen garden, in the words of John and Nancy Todd, two of the founders of the New Alchemy Institute, "wildness and wilderness must be revered and tentacles of wildness allowed to permeate, like the threads of a tapestry."

The Soil Garden

On Shelter Island, not too far from where we live, there's a street called Menhaden Lane, which runs down to Gardiner's Bay. The street gets its name from the menhaden fish, a member of the herring family that was once found in huge schools in local waters. The remains of countless menhaden have been transformed, in the same process of death and renewal that goes on almost everywhere in nature, into the soils that mantle Shelter Island and the oaks and sassafras trees of the forests that now grow again on former farmland.

Shelter Islanders, like many early New England farmers, used menhaden in a mixture with manure to make the compost that kept their lands fertile. A layer of manure about a foot high was spread on the ground, followed by a layer of fish. Alternating layers of manure and fish continued to be applied until the pile reached a height of five or six feet, at which point it was topped off with a final layer of manure.

Shelter Island farmers knew that topsoil, with its living matrix of minerals, microorganisms, organic matter, and invertebrates, was the backbone of the land. But when the sons and daughters of New England settlers trekked westward in search of inexpensive acreage, they found soil that was unfathomably rich in organic matter left by centuries of decayed prairie grasses and forbs and bison droppings, and they gave little further thought to renewing the earth with compost. Modern agriculture and horticulture, built on a disregard for soil, were thus born.

When undisturbed by human activities, soil is usually covered by a protective canopy of trees, shrubs, or grasses, and is constantly being renewed as dead leaves decay. Modern cultivation techniques lay bare the soil to the erosive forces of wind and water and break the cycle of decay and renewal. Soil is lost much faster than it is created.

By 1976, American farmers were losing an estimated six tons of soil for every ton of grain they produced. Farmers in Iowa, whose rich prairie soils comprise the greatest concentration of prime farmland in the country, have already destroyed half their topsoil, and nationwide, almost half of this country's cropland is losing soil faster than it can be replaced. One survey measured our annual soil loss at 3.1 billion tons—a rate approaching that seen during the Dust Bowl years.

In developing countries, the situation is even worse: erosion rates are twice as high as in the United States, partly because exploding human populations mean the land must be more intensively farmed. A 1978 dispatch from the U.S. embassy in Addis Ababa indicated that an estimated one billion tons of topsoil were washing down from Ethiopia's highlands every year, presaging the devastating famines that have followed. Worldwide, farmers are losing an estimated twenty-four billion tons of topsoil each year. New topsoil is constantly being formed, of course, but at nature's own leisurely pace.

When chemical fertilizers made their debut in American agriculture, around 1950, manufacturers promised that the highly concentrated nutrients synthesized from fossil fuels would replenish the incredible richness that had been stored in the soil over thousands of years and depleted in about five decades. Almost half a century later, this promise remains unfulfilled. In the absence of the cover crops used by farmers and gardeners through the centuries to prevent erosion and return organic matter to the land, soil continues to erode away. What's more, the concentrated fertilizers and poisonous pesticides have destroyed many of the microorganisms and earthworms that are so critical to natural cycles of soil renewal.

Ignoring the natural nutrient cycle causes other ecological harms as well. Every time we rake leaves or lawn clippings, deadhead, or prune, and then bag it up and leave it on the curb, we're contributing to that enormous environmental problem known as "municipal solid waste." According to the Environmental Protection Agency, yard trimmings account for almost 20 percent of what ends up in landfills—about 31 million tons a year. If kitchen food scraps are added in, the total comes to about 30 percent.

Much of our difficulty with waste is embedded in the word itself: waste is a human invention. Natural systems, unlike modern human ones, have a kind of thrift, a built-in recycling ability. Nature handles every form of waste—fallen leaves, for example— by turning it into food for another generation of plants and animals.

The legacy of a British government agronomist named Sir Albert Howard has helped us relearn what peasant farmers have known for centuries, that we need somehow to put back into the soil everything our plants take out. Sir Albert spent thirty years, from 1905 to 1934, in India, where he developed modern organic gardening. At the time, a shortage of fuel had forced India's poor to begin using dried dung as a fuel for cooking, thus severely decreasing the amount of manure returned yearly to the soil. To replace a part of this lost manure, Sir Albert devised the so-called Indore method of making humus, primarily out of plant remains: materials are stacked in layers and then turned, or mixed by earthworms, during the decomposition process. He found by experimenting that the best compost consisted of three times as much plant matter as manure.

Sir Albert gave credit for the basic ideas on which he built his compost piles to the Chinese, who had long managed to keep their soil in a high state of fertility even as it supported an enormous population. They achieved this by carefully returning all organic remains to the land.

Organic gardeners of the 1960s and '70s strove to bring the work of Sir Albert to the American middle class, but their zeal to convince the rest of the country of the virtues and healing powers of, the magic surrounding, and the essential ecological need for composting resulted in the technique's being viewed as the horticultural equivalent of oat bran, practiced almost exclusively by bearded hippies in rumpled flannel shirts. People really thought organic gardeners had gone off the deep end when a small vanguard began to champion the composting or waterless toilet as a way of transforming that final frontier of potential nutrients, human excrement, into well-aged, pathogen-free compost to be used in the landscape, and all without wasting a drop of precious water for flushing. A few staunch advocates continue to sing the praises of composting privies even today, but these toilets are expensive, and most users have found them to be, to put it delicately, a pain in the neck. While composting toilets may be necessary in areas where water supplies are extremely limited, to most Americans they seem rather draconian, especially with the newfound availability of cheap, reliable toilets that use a mere one and a half gallons per flush, and the development of more ecologically sensible methods of sewage treatment.

WHAT HAPPENS IN a compost heap in a garden is simply a speeded-up version of one of the fundamental processes that go on every day in every forest, every thicket, every meadow, every swamp and bog in the world. The cycling of nutrients is a vital function of every natural community. In a healthy, stable ecosystem, most nutrients are recycled internally; they don't come from somewhere else. And most of the nutrients are recycled via the decomposition of litter, the fallen remains of plants and other living organisms.

Millions of years ago, bacteria transformed the Earth from a cratered, moonlike terrain of rock into the fertile globe we know. Toothless and mouthless, these microorganisms ingested through their membranes and then chemically digested the hard, bare rock of the planet, laying down their carcasses to produce a living soil of humus in which the earliest plants could become established. Today, the descendants of these microorganisms continue to ensure the earth's fertility by recycling the remains of plants and animals and converting them into humus, which provides a secure supply of continually available nutrients for plant growth.

Rates of natural decomposition vary. In the boreal forests of the northern regions—for example, the jack pine forests of northern Canada—organic material decomposes very slowly, with some elements taking as long as sixteen years to recycle. In sharp contrast, litter in tropical rain forests decomposes quickly, with almost a complete turnover occurring every year. Decomposition rates in the deciduous forests of temperate zones fall somewhere between these two extremes.

The glacial pace of natural decomposition just isn't fast enough to sustain the modern, human-dominated landscape: because in some parts of the garden, especially the kitchen garden, we cultivate so intensively, we can't wait for nature to take its course. The nutrient needs of crops such as tomatoes, squash, and strawberries are so enormous that ordinary processes of decomposition could never meet them. But it's possible to speed up natural processes of decomposition and create humus via composting in as little as a few weeks.

Although thousands of different kinds of microorganisms are at work at any given time in a healthy compost pile, they can all be divided into three main groups. Unless you're starting a pile in the middle of the summer, when temperatures are high, the first wave of microbial activity will typically be undertaken by cool-temperature bacteria called psychrophiles, which perform most efficiently at about fifty-five degrees Fahrenheit. These bacteria start digesting the organic matter and releasing nutrients in the form of amino acids. Because heat is a byproduct of bacterial metabolism, the pile now begins to heat up.

As the temperature of the compost pile rises, it becomes less hospitable to the cool-loving psychrophiles, and the mesophilic bacteria take over. These microbes, which are most comfortable at about seventy to ninety degrees Fahrenheit, accomplish most of the work of decomposition in a compost heap. If you start your pile in midsummer, when air temperatures are consistently in their preferred range, the mesophiles will pitch in right away, eliminating the psychrophilic process altogether.

If and when the mesophiles heat the pile up to about a hundred degrees Fahrenheit, the thermophiles step in. These bacteria can raise the temperature to as high as 160 degrees before it stabilizes. Unless new material is constantly added to a pile and it is turned at strategic times, the thermophilic phase will last only a few days. Psychrophilic, mesophilic, or thermophilic bacteria will continue metabolizing the organic matter until either they are replaced by some other kind of microorganism or there is nothing left for them to consume.

Other forms of life are active in the compost pile, too: fungi break down tough cellulose and lignin, while actinomycetes, identifiable as the grayish, cobweblike material in the pile, help the fungi decompose whatever cellulose, starches, proteins, and lignin the bacteria leave behind. Earthworms also play an important role, aerating the pile as they digest the materials and deposit nutrient-rich castings.

Just as humus formation does in nature, compost enhances the cycling of nutrients in a garden. The rich, dark particles of compost coat particles of sand, silt, and clay in the soil to form small aggregates, or crumbs, that improve soil structure, water storage, and pore space, and therefore aeration. Finished compost contains nutrients that plants need to grow, such as nitrogen, phosphorus, and potassium. It's an especially good supplier of the micronutrients needed in small quantities, including boron, iodine, manganese, and molybdenum. The more varied the materials used to make compost, the greater the variety of nutrients it will provide. In some situations, in fact, soil enriched by compost may not need any additional fertilizer.

Another bonus is that the nutrients in compost are released at precisely the rate that plants need them. Early in the season, when plants are just beginning to grow, the microorganisms in compost are slowly releasing nutrients. As the weather warms up and the plants begin their growth spurts, the microbes work faster, producing more nutrients. And there's another bonus, too: soluble plant nutrients that might otherwise leach through the soil and out of the reach of plant roots are held in place by compost. In short, compost not only provides important nutrients but also helps the garden ecosystem conserve and use them more efficiently.

In the soil garden, we address serious environmental problems by acknowledging the importance of nature's nutrient cycle. By devoting a small portion of the yard to composting, we can allow natural processes of decomposition to transform waste into food for the plants that support all life—and by returning it to the soil, we can help renew the Earth.

The Water Garden

Whereas in the soil garden we acknowledge the importance of nature's nutrient cycle, in the water garden we celebrate nature's hydrologic cycle. In the water garden we shape the landscape to stabilize water flow and reduce polluting runoff, and at the same

time create beautiful backyard wetlands that can become important wildlife habitat.

The water cycle is one of nature's more elegant inventions.
The cycle begins as the sun's energy warms the surface waters
of oceans, lakes, and rivers. Some of this water evaporates, rising
up to the atmosphere, where it forms clouds of water vapor.
When the clouds cool, the water vapor condenses, then falls to
the earth as rain or snow, supporting every terrestrial creature
before ultimately rejoining the seas and lakes, where the cycle
begins anew.

When water falling from the sky reaches the ground, it follows three main paths. Some of it is absorbed into the topsoil,
where it may be intercepted and used by plants. In this case it is
returned to the atmosphere through evapotranspiration, or the
evaporation of water from land surfaces plus transpiration, the
water given off by the roots and leaves of plants. Other precipitation seeps down through the soil to replenish underground
aquifers. Finally, when the rate or amount of precipitation
exceeds the speed at which it can be absorbed by the soil or used
by plants, the excess water, called runoff, flows off the land and
collects in wetlands, lakes, and rivers, which eventually flow to
the sea.

Over the centuries, the water cycle has left its imprint on
the Earth, etching a vast web of watersheds into the planet's
surface. A watershed encompasses all of the land that drains into
a single river or other body of water. A small creek that runs
through one part of a watershed may seem to be unrelated
to a stream that flows miles away, but if they belong to the same
watershed, they are connected. Creeks join together to create
larger streams, which in turn form rivers, in a natural drainage
network that today carries rainwater from gardens, farms,
and roads into estuaries, bays, lakes, and other major bodies
of water.

In a natural landscape—a pristine forest, for example—there is generally little runoff. The soil and its dense cover of vegetation act as a sponge, absorbing most precipitation. However, as we humans have radically altered the natural hydrologic cycle, by reshaping entire watersheds and replacing the natural vegetative cover with roofs, driveways, streets, and parking lots, the Earth's surface has become much more impervious. Rainfall no longer soaks into the soil as readily as it once did; even the lawn we've planted across forty million acres of North America has a low infiltration rate. The net result is that the volume of storm-water runoff has vastly increased. The system of concrete pipes and channels that we've devised to carry runoff has also multiplied the rate at which these potential torrents of water flow into creeks and streams, causing flooding and erosion. The soil scoured away from stream-sides and riverbanks is deposited downstream or in lakes and reservoirs, displacing water and precipitating even more flooding. Water quality is also affected: the storm water that rolls off our roofs and lawns and down our driveways and streets to storm drains collects fertilizers, pesticides, motor oil, and pet wastes on its way to streams and rivers, where it can cause extensive environmental damage.

Meanwhile, wetlands—the ecosystems that have evolved over the ages to contain excess rainwater (thereby decreasing the likelihood and severity of floods), break down pollutants, and replenish groundwater—are our most imperiled habitats. It's estimated that only about 99 million out of the 215 million acres of wetlands that existed in the contiguous forty-eight states two hundred years ago remain intact today.

Vast freshwater marshes, or wetlands featuring mostly herbaceous vegetation, once ranged from the sawgrass expanses of Florida's Everglades to the wetland prairies of Georgia's Okefenokee to the wet meadows of New England, home to great blue herons, muskrats, and moose. The prairie pothole region, extending from the north-central United States into south-central Canada, was formerly peppered with marshes cloaking the thousands of depressions that were formed ten thousand years ago, during the last Ice Age. Peatlands—wetlands in which organic matter decomposes so slowly that it continually builds up—were common in Minnesota and Maine, with smaller pockets located in the Pacific Northwest, the western mountains, and the Appalachian Mountains in West Virginia. Such boreal wetlands are still widespread in Canada, which, with more than six hundred thousand square miles, has the highest concentration of peatlands in the world. Swamps, or wetlands studded with trees and shrubs, also covered huge acreages, from the cypress swamps of the South and the floodplain swamps of the Mississippi valley to the pocosins in the Carolinas, the red-maple swamps in the East, and the spruce, tamarack, and cedar swamps of the northern United States and Canada.

California has already done away with 91 percent of its original five million acres of wetlands. Iowa has lost 98 percent of its prairie potholes, Minnesota 75 percent, and North Dakota 49 percent. Yet acre for acre, prairie potholes support the greatest variety and number of animals of any biological community in North America. The fastest-drying of these wetland depressions are the first to warm in spring, providing an invertebrate soup for protein-starved waterfowl arriving from their winter ranges. Later, as these seasonal wetlands dry up, migrant shorebirds feast on the fauna in the exposed mudflats. These and most other wetlands are in fact among the Earth's richest ecosystems in terms of their biological output, of both plant and animal life, rivaling even the most fertile farmlands in their productivity.

All the while that we've been draining wetlands, we've also been using water prodigiously. According to the Environmental

Protection Agency, the average American family of four uses 243 gallons of water indoors every day—more than twice the amount used by the typical European family. That figure doesn't even take into account the water used outdoors, yet we know that our yards, especially our lawns, can soak up as much as 50 percent of the total water consumed by the average family. As the human population in many areas has surpassed nature's capacity to supply enough fresh water via precipitation, elaborate water projects have been constructed to pipe in water from remote watersheds, often hundreds of miles away. In other areas, such as Long Island, fossil water deposited in aquifers over thousands of years is rapidly being depleted.

In recent years, gardeners have become attuned to the need to conserve water. We've invested in water-saving technologies such as drip irrigation and learned how to mulch to discourage water in the soil from evaporating into the air. We're also starting to accept the fact that some plants simply aren't suited to the precipitation patterns in our areas, and to limit our plant palettes accordingly. In other words, we're beginning to realize that our gardens should be designed to rely solely on rainfall, fog drip, and snow melt. Still, the flip side of the solution to our water problems—the notion that our gardens should be designed to prevent polluted water from ever leaving our property—has yet to sink in.

Not long ago, Don and I did some minor calculations to figure out how much water rolls off the roof of our summer cottage on Shelter Island every year. We weren't worried about losing all this precious water that might otherwise be diverted to irrigating the garden; our low-maintenance natural landscape of woodland and meadow plants doesn't require any supplemental water, except for the new transplants we add from time to time. However, every time it rained—and Shelter Island gets its share of dramatic downpours—storm water would come gushing down the roof gutters, and in the front of the house, all that runoff was creating a small gully and carrying eroding soil down our unpaved driveway. Water from the back gutters was meanwhile collecting in a shallow depression right behind the house, seeping into the crawl space, and causing moisture problems.

According to our calculations, over twenty thousand gallons of water pour off the roof each year. We pondered the best way to integrate this water into the natural hydrologic cycle. If we lived in a drier climate, where it was essential to collect every available drop of water, we might have considered building a cistern, a tank located in the basement or underground to store runoff from the roof. But our problem wasn't too little water, it was too much. In our case, the optimal solution would prevent polluting runoff and erosion by allowing the storm water to percolate slowly through the soil and into the water table—preferably in some way that would eliminate the moisture problems under the house.

After exploring the alternatives, we decided to build a rock-filled dry well at the base of the downspot in front of the house. In this area, only a driveway about fifteen feet wide separates the structure from the surrounding forest, so our options were limited. Because even this excavation couldn't contain all the water dropped by the hurricanes and nor'easters that regularly pummel the island, we also dug a trench that leads from the dry well down the driveway, and filled it, too, with rocks. During major storms, runoff can now flow down the dry well as well as down the long, narrow drainage trench and then percolate down through the subsoil. Both the dry well and the trench are topped with sand and a layer of the small beach stones that can be found all over the island (Shelter Island, like larger, nearby Long Island, is basically a pile of rocks deposited at the southern terminus of the last glacier). These same stones cover the entire driveway, the path to the front door, and the patio behind the house; unlike asphalt and other types of impermeable paving, which are major contributors to urban and suburban runoff, they enable storm water to soak into the ground and thence into the water table.

In the back of the house, where there is a little more cleared land, we decided to create an artificial marsh. We excavated a fifteen-by-five-foot area along the back of the house, nine inches out from the foundation and about three feet deep, and lined it with a single, unbroken plastic liner. Then we filled the hole with a mixture of half compost and half excavated soil.

Now, any storm water that drips from where the gutter sections connect along the eaves falls into our created wetland. A length of flexible plastic pipe connected to a downspout at the back of the house carries roof runoff to this wetland as well. To keep our wetland garden from overflowing during serious storms, we poked drainage holes in the side of the liner opposite the house, about a foot below the soil surface.

This southwest-facing area behind the house gets a few hours of sunlight in the afternoon before the setting sun dips behind the nearby trees—just enough sunshine to support a decent variety of flowering plants. This gave me a great excuse to create the wetland garden I've always wanted. A range of fascinating plants, from turtleheads and sedges to dewdrops and pitcher plants, are native to wetland environments; because I was determined that our backyard wetland should attract native butterflies and ruby-throated hummingbirds, I choose only plants that were indigenous to freshwater marshes on Shelter Island. The spectacular pink, four-to-six-inch-wide, saucer-shaped blooms of swamp mallow, the fragrant white flowers of sweet pepperbush, the massive, dusty pink flowerheads of Joe-pye weed, and the dark purple-red flowers of New York ironweed loom over the wetland garden in late summer, following the blue flowers of blueflag iris with their intricate yellow and purple veining, the pink and white turtleheads, and the colorful flower spikes of blue and red lobelia. The wetland wildflowers mingle with tussocks of

Wetland plants, including soft rush (Juncus effusus),
arrow arum (Peltandra virginica),
ironweed (Vernonia noveboracensis),
Joe-pye weed (Eupatorium maculatum),
and swamp mallow (Hibiscus moscheutos).

soft rush and palm sedge and the fleshy, arrowhead-shaped leaves of arrow arum.

Our miniature marsh satisfies the needs of brilliant butterflies and moths, peepers, frogs, birds, and other wildlife. At the same time, the runoff that flows off the roof and into the dry well in our driveway helps replenish the underground reservoir that provides the fresh, pure drinking water that supports our house's human inhabitants.

The Machine in the Garden

WHEN I WAS in college, English majors were supposed to swoon over the geniuses of Western (meaning, European) literature. I, however, gravitated more toward rustic Americans such as Whitman and Thoreau. It wasn't until I read the literary critic Leo Marx that I realized why I was so drawn to American writers. In his classic dissertation on the pastoral ideal in American literature, Marx writes, "Americans, so far as they shared an idea of what they were doing as a people, actually saw themselves creating a society in the image of a *garden*" (emphasis mine).

Marx's book *The Machine in the Garden* explores how American writers from Washington Irving to F. Scott Fitzgerald grappled with the theme of the pastoral, that vision of human culture in harmony with a beneficent nature which has been traced back through Western history to ancient Rome, and especially to the poet Virgil. The pastoral ideal, Marx argues, has been used to define the meaning of America since the age of discovery. The ruling motive was the desire to escape from the decadent world and begin a new life in a fresh, green landscape. "And now here was a virgin continent!" he notes. "Inevitably the European mind was dazzled by the prospect."

American writers invented new forms for the pastoral. Instead of extolling Virgil's Arcadia, they sang the praises of the wild terrain of the North American continent. Instead of enlisting gentle shepherds, they peopled the New World's landscape with farmers and other scrappy, independent types. Instead of using the highfalutin language of pastoral poetry, they employed the exuberant idiom of the working man.

Yet our version of the pastoral always seems to go awry.

For me, the most haunting examination of the American pastoral myth is F. Scott Fitzgerald's *The Great Gatsby*, published in 1925. Gatsby is a Midwesterner who has come east to make his fortune. From the start, Nick Carraway, Gatsby's next-door neighbor and fellow Midwesterner (and Fitzgerald's narrator), realizes that there is something false about the pastoral ideal embodied by the mansions and elegant green lawns of their adopted home, suburban Long Island's Gold Coast. Describing his first impression of one of these suburban manses, Nick says that the "lawn started at the beach and ran toward the front door for a quarter of a mile, jumping over sun-dials and brick walks and burning gardens—finally when it reached the house drifting up the side in bright vines as though from the momentum of its run."

Eventually, Nick comes to understand the connection between this seemingly bucolic suburban landscape and the industrial landscape that was engulfing America by the Roaring Twenties. He realizes that the monstrous technological wilderness he passes during his daily commutes to Manhattan is in fact the truer emblem of the rich and powerful society that makes possible Gatsby's wealth, his lavish parties, and his most prized possession, the flashy car that is ultimately the instrument of his demise. Who can forget Nick's description of this desolate area, "a valley of ashes—a fantastic farm where ashes grow like wheat into ridges and hills and grotesque gardens; where ashes take the forms of houses and chimneys and rising smoke and, finally, with a transcendent effort, of men who move dimly and already crumbling through the powdery air"?

In the final pages of the book, the night after Gatsby's death, Nick sprawls on the beach, gazing out onto the Long Island Sound. The summer is over. What he sees at last enables him to explain the mysterious, transcendent quality not only of Gatsby but also of the culture that produced him, a culture peculiarly susceptible to pastoral illusions. Nick observes that

> most of the big shore places were closed now and there were hardly any lights except the shadowy, moving glow of a ferryboat across the Sound. And as the moon rose higher the inessential houses began to melt away until gradually I became aware of the old island here that flowered once for Dutch sailors' eyes—a great green breast of the new world. Its vanished trees, the trees that had made way for Gatsby's house, had once pandered in whispers to the last and greatest of all human dreams; for a transitory enchanted moment man must have held his breath in the presence of this continent . . . face to face for the last time in history with something commensurate to his capacity for wonder.

So what does Nick do? He decides to leave New York, the epicenter of turn-of-the-century American civilization, and go back west—for Americans, the direction of nature. Like countless other heroes of American fiction, he comes to understand the tragic limits of the pastoral dream, yet is compelled nonetheless to head westward, toward the simpler Midwestern landscape of his youth, a pastoral landscape that even then had already largely vanished.

Like Faulkner, Hemingway, West, and other twentieth-century American writers, Fitzgerald invoked the traditional image of America as an unspoiled landscape redolent of possibility. But at the same time, all of these writers recognized the power of the machine or of some other symbol of the counter-force that has stripped the old pastoral ideal of most of its meaning. Today, if we look back across the great gulf created by industrialism, Marx suggests that we can see that the endings to the great masterpieces of American literature never seem quite satisfactory because their take on America embodies a naive and ultimately static view of history. Our pastoral dream doesn't encompass the restless striving of human beings, and the old symbols of reconciliation between nature and culture have therefore become obsolete. "To change the situation," Marx believes, "we require new symbols of possibility."

A FEW CONTEMPORARY thinkers see the American garden, as opposed to the unspoiled wilderness of the frontier, as this new symbol of possibility. In virgin wilderness, we're forever condemned to be ecological outlaws; as the Sierra Club motto admonishes, when we step into the wilderness, we should "take only photos, leave only footprints," because only nature untouched by human hands is "pure." By contrast, at its best a garden is a place where we nurture nature as nature nurtures us; in the garden we can redefine our role in nature, act out a healthier relationship with the rest of nature on a daily basis.

The restoration ecologist William R. Jordan III has done more than anyone to develop this idea in a series of graceful essays published in the journal *Restoration & Management Notes*. In Jordan's view, ecological restoration will prove to be a major component of the American garden, and an essential element of the distinctively American relationship with nature. The restoration of ancient ecosystems such as the tallgrass prairie, he says, is in some sense a search for a vanished Eden, just like the adventures of Huck Finn or Jay Gatsby. But whereas the heroes of American literature are forced to deny history and change, the restorationist is forced to confront them: by attempting to reverse ecological damage, he or she learns the hard lessons of history and the necessity of discriminating between healthy actions and destructive ones. The resulting widsom, Jordan maintains, is a crucial aspect of our emerging relationship with non-human nature.

Jordan contrasts this new way of thinking with the brand of environmentalism that urges us to discard modern knowledge and live, as indigenous cultures are believed to have done, in a gentle, unself-conscious harmony with the world around us. This view, he writes, "minimizes the classic role of humans as gatherers, as predators, and as shapers of the landscape." Built on a much different conception of the natural relationship between humans and nature, the new ecological paradigm holds that there has always been a distinction, even a "measure of estrangement," between us and the rest of nature, and that this is not some monstrous consequence of the invention of monotheism or the scientific revolution, as some have suggested, but simply a result of our being human, of having a higher level of self-awareness than other creatures.

According to Jordan, ecological restoration offers us an ideal framework in which to work out the terms of our relationship with nature. It is capable of leading us back *into* nature, "without demanding, impossibly, that we 'back up' historically, or cease to be who we are, and who we have become."

Jordan has written that perhaps the most important thing restoration can contribute to environmentalism is not merely its products, but also the process of active participation in the ecology of the land community. For him, this process comprises the constant study of natural systems and our effects upon them, a continual doing and undoing as we recognize our adverse impacts and take steps to compensate for them.

A small but growing number of gardeners is taking this notion quite literally. In their view, the restoration of native plants is the be-all and end-all of contemporary horticulture, and planting exotics is a form of environmental treason.

You'd think that gardeners would be the last to succumb to such false modesty. We have, after all, been responsible, both intentionally and unintentionally, for the expansion of diversity that is so evident in the development of both food and ornamental crops. And in some ways we're producing ever more diversity, ever faster. It took centuries for us to create the many vegetable varieties, from cabbages to cauliflower to collards, resulting from the single species *Brassica oleracea*. But in a matter of only decades, beginning with the crossing of the yellow trumpet narcissus with the flat-flowered poet's narcissus (of the red-rimmed eye) in the quest for a narcissus with an orange trumpet, we've developed enough new daffodil hybrids to support an entire garden industry. Today, hundreds of narcissus cultivars are grouped into no fewer than twelve divisions based on their flower form, from the large-cup daffodils with their large trumpets and one flower per stalk to the tazettas with their four to eight single or double flowers per stem.

Don't get me wrong: I'm convinced of the need for ecological restoration in the home garden as well as in the larger landscape. But I don't think people will—or should—be content simply to re-create the plant communities of the past.

All those natural landscapers who believe that any horticultural creation other than a faithful reproduction of a native plant community is at best frivolous and at worst destructive must be unfamiliar with the work of John Todd. An aquatic biologist, Todd is developing ecologically engineered systems in greenhouses—essentially, indoor gardens—made up of a series of functional aquatic and wetland habitats, none of which existed in

A variety of narcissi.

nature until he invented it. His creations, which he calls Living Machines, are already being used in some homes and commercial structures to turn sewage into pure water.

Wastewater is one of the most massive pollutant loads produced by the modern home. Polluted water from sinks, dishwashers, and toilets has to go *somewhere*. If you live in a rural area, it ends up in a septic tank on your property; the excess then flows to an underground leach field, where soil organisms break down the pollutants. Contaminated water can sometimes reach underground water supplies, and every few years, the septic tank will need to be pumped out. The septage is trucked to a "treatment" facility, often consisting of a series of primitive settling ponds or lagoons. In large towns and cities, wastewater is piped to a sewage-treatment plant. The effluent discharged from these facilities typically remains full of nitrogen and phosphorus that pollute receiving waterways. By contrast, in homes outfitted with Todd's Living Machines, no contaminated wastewater leaves the site: all sewage is virtually purified in these indoor gardens—not just partially treated, as in the typical treatment plant, but actually *purified*—and recycled back into the house. The frontiers of this new indoor gardening are still largely unexplored.

A few years ago, I toured the Living Machine installed at the Field's Point Wastewater Treatment Facility, located in the industrial bowels of Providence, at the top of Narragansett Bay. This experimental Living Machine can handle sixteen thousand gallons of sewage a day, or the amount produced by about 120 households. Inside the 30-by-120-foot greenhouse, a wooden walkway bisects four rows of translucent plastic cylinders. Each row of thirteen-hundred-gallon cylinders is connected in a series. Todd describes these as a "series of microcosms"—whole, self-contained ecosystems designed to mimic larger global cycles, such as the food chain. The series of microcosms supports all the species necessary to remove both nutrients and toxins from the water.

When raw sewage flows into the first cylinder, ancient forms of life, such as the bacteria found in any eutrophic pond, begin the process of breaking down the pollutants. The bacteria consume the nutrient-laden organic matter from the wastewater and convert toxic ammonia to nitrite and nitrate, food for plants. Some of the nitrate is ingested by algae growing on the sides of the cylinders, and the algae in turn is grazed upon by snails. Zooplankton meanwhile feed on the algae suspended in the wastewater—"and on and on churns the natural food chain cycle of an ecologically engineered system, purifying the wastewater with each step," in the words of John Todd.

Fish and higher plants also play significant roles in the food chains of Todd's Living Machines. The water hyacinth (*Eichhornia crassipes*), a floating aquatic plant, consumes pollutants in the first five cylinders. Other aquatics, including parrot's feather (*Myriophyllum aquaticum*), duckweeds (*Lemna*, *Spirodela*, and *Wolffia* species) and water velvets (*Azolla* species), are spread throughout the remaining containers, where they form dense mats. Still other aquatics, such as watercress, grow on a mesh of screens rafted on the surface of the tanks. More than one hundred different terrestrial plants, both temperate and tropical in origin, have been tested in the unique aquatic environment of the water surface; members of the mint and ginger families have done particularly well. Even some trees, such as the bald cypress, thrive in this novel habitat. Several species of bulrush, papyrus, and other plants grow in two rows of engineered marshes, one at the midpoint of the process and another—this one a final "polishing" marsh—at the very end. In the second half of the treatment process, fish such as the golden shiner, one of New England's primary bait fish, thrive on the internal food chains and spawn among the surface plants each spring.

When he first started experimenting with Living Machines, Todd grew mostly cattails, bulrushes, and other traditional wetland plants. Now he uses anything and everything, from ornamental grasses to tomatoes. My pulse races when I think about what a great landscape designer could do with one of these indoor gardens!

What Todd calls the seeding of a Living Machine is critical because the bioengineered system relies on ecological diversity for its resiliency, self-repair, and overall efficiency. What he has in mind is a diversity not just of individual species but also of communities: diverse microbial communities to provide a range of metabolic functions, diverse communities of photosynthesizing plants to utilize sunlight, and diverse phyla, from bacteria to vertebrates, to fill all available ecological niches.

The Providence facility, for example, was established with repeated "seedings" from natural environments as well as with commercially cultured bacteria and microorganisms from the adjacent, conventional sewage-treatment facility. These initial seedings contained organisms from more than a dozen environments, including the intertidal zones of a Cape Cod salt marsh, brackish salt ponds, a vernal pond, and southern New England streams—some 150 species of protozoans and two dozen species of snails alone. According to Todd, as the ecosystems developed, natural selection proceeded rapidly. Many species disappeared, while others proved highly adapted and not only survived but also flourished. Microscopic investigation of the photosynthetic communities attached to the walls of the translucent cylinders has revealed an extraordinary richness and complexity, in "sandwichlike" community structures with different combinations of bacteria, algae, and protozoans, depending on their location in the treatment process.

Over the past twenty-five years, Todd and his associates have designed and built Living Machines that grow food, heat and cool buildings, and treat sewage, septage, sludge, and other wastes. These wastes, as well as other forms of pollution—such as alterations in the mix of atmospheric gases that controls the global climate—are, like the loss of biological diversity, Todd says, "artifacts of technological cultures estranged from the great natural systems of the planet." Finding ways to integrate advanced societies such as ours with the natural world, to the benefit of both, is one of the great tasks of our time. This new symbiotic relationship between humans and nature, Todd thinks, will be predicated on innovative, highly evolved ecological technologies such as Living Machines.

FOR GOOD AND for ill, under our influence, evolution is accelerating quickly. There has been a rapid evolution not only of plants and animals and, now, new ecological communities under domestication, but also of weeds in greatly disturbed wild habitats. What does it all portend? For more than half a century, there has been intense speculation that the disturbances we humans are visiting on the planet are leading to increasing hybridization in the wild, and that the new habitats we leave in our wake and the countless new hybrids they support are all part of an evolutionary upheaval of our own making.

In 1947, the botanist Edgar Anderson wrote a fascinating essay on this subject, entitled "The Hybridization of the Habitat." At the time, most biologists believed that hybridization between species was rare in nature; the prevailing opinion held that hybrids were so seldom found because most organisms produced by the crossing of two different species were sterile. Anderson, however, marshalled an impressive amount of evidence to the contrary, compiled by geneticists, by taxonomists, and especially by plant breeders. After all, if horticulturists could produce hundreds of new varieties by crossing two narcissus species, why shouldn't nature be able—and even more apt—to do this sort of thing in the wild?

In his essay, published in the journal *Evolution*, Anderson argued that hybridization was indeed occurring in nature, but that the natural hybrids went unrecorded because they left no apparent descendants, except under the most unusual conditions. One reason natural hybridization was so seldom seen, he hypothesized, was that when hybrids did develop, they usually perpetuated themselves, if at all, in backcrosses to whichever parent species was the more abundant. The progeny of these secondary hybrids likewise crossed back again, and on and on. Anderson coined a term for this process: introgressive hybridization. The ordinary biologist would not be able to distinguish between the parent species and the "mongrel nature of their descendants," yet such hybridization, he asserted, by providing the means for the mixing of genes between the two lines, resulted in the enrichment of variation in the participating species. Today, some fifty years later, new genetic screening technologies such as electrophoresis have begun to corroborate an unusual frequency of rare gene combinations in areas where hybrids proliferate.

In his essay, Anderson went on to suggest that yet another reason hybrids were so rarely found in nature is that the hybrid generations require their own peculiar habitats, which under ordinary natural conditions don't exist. He used two species of spiderwort that grow wild in the Ozarks as an example. One, *Tradescantia subaspera*, thrives in deep, rich woods at the foot of bluffs, while the other, *T. canaliculata*, grows up above in full sun at the edge of the cliffs. Anderson was able to find precious few first-generation hybrids in the wild, though they crossed readily in an experimental garden. This he attributed to the fact that in all of the Ozark Plateau, there was little or none of the intermediate habitat—gravelly soil with a light covering of leaf litter in partial shade—required for the hybrid's survival.

Imagine what would happen if these first-generation hybrids

crossed, Anderson wrote. Taking into consideration only the three habitat characteristics mentioned above (the actual number of differences between the two species is much greater), he calculated that their offspring, with their reshuffled sets of genes, would require six new habitats in addition to the parents' two:

rich loam	*rocky soil*
full sun	*deep shade*
no leaf mold	*leaf mold*
rich loam	*rocky soil*
full sun	*full sun*
leaf mold	*leaf mold*
rich loam	*rocky soil*
deep shade	*deep shade*
no leaf mold	*no leaf mold*

Anderson emphasized that the number of different kinds of habitats demanded by the hybrids would rise exponentially with the number of basic differences between the different species. "With ten such differences," he wrote, "around a thousand different kinds of habitat would be needed to permit the various recombinations to find a niche. . . . With only twenty such basic differences (and this seems like a conservative figure) over a million different recombined habitats would be needed."

Under natural conditions, this would be virtually impossible. Only the kind of ecological havoc caused by humans could create the strange new habitats necessary for the survival of the bizarre new hybrid combinations. Anderson came up with a new term for our transformation of the planet: the hybridization of the habitat.

Anderson cited other botanists whose work buttressed his

own assertion that humans were providing new niches for hybrid combinations. In the Mississippi Delta, for example, different hybrids of two conspicuously different irises, *Iris fulva* and *I. giganticaerulea*, were found on farms treated somewhat differently by their respective owners. One farm in particular had a "swarm of different hybrid derivatives, almost like an experimental garden, and the hybrid area went right up to the fenceline at the border of the farm and stopped there."

Six years later, in an article titled "Hybridization as an Evolutionary Stimulus," Anderson and his coauthor G. L. Stebbins, Jr., came to an even more breathtaking conclusion. They pointed to new studies showing that evolution had proceeded not by slow, even steps but rather in bursts of creative activity. This was what had happened during the Cretaceous period, for example, when overgrazing by the dinosaurs, among other factors, led to, in Anderson and Stebbins's words, "the greatest revolution in vegetation that the world has ever seen"—the replacement of conifers and other gymnosperms with the flowering plants that predominate today. This kind of thing happened whenever new oceanic islands were colonized by seeds blown in on the wind or carried by seabirds, as in Hawaii and the Galapagos, with their unique and novel floras and faunas. This was, moreover, what had happened most recently during the Pleistocene era, when massive ice sheets scoured the continents of the Northern Hemisphere. In the strange new sets of habitats thus created, Anderson and Stebbins surmised, some hybrids must have been at a selective advantage. Hybridization in these disturbed habitats in turn produced the conditions under which the more familiar evolutionary processes such as mutation and selection could proceed at top speed. Disturbance and the resulting hybridization could thus have been responsible for the resulting "quantum evolution," or extraordinary bursts of natural creativity.

*Primitive forms of monkey-puzzles and cycadlike plants
that would have been found during the dinosaur
era, at the dawn of the age of flowering plants.*

This, the authors concluded, is what we are seeing right now. At the moment, it is we who are the ecological dominants. It is we, they wrote, who are "having a catastrophic effect upon the world's faunas and floras." We are doing what the dinosaurs did before us, only faster. According to Anderson and Stebbins, "The enhanced evolution which we see in our own gardens, dooryards, dumps, and roadsides may well be typical of what happened during the rise of previous ecological dominants."

There's one big difference, though: the dinosaurs didn't know what they were doing, and we do.

And so we are left with a momentous choice. We can "shed modern knowledge," renounce our intellectual gifts, and, by deigning *not* to do whatever is in our power to stop the growing torrent of extinctions, let evolution proceed on its current course—come what may for us as well as for the other creatures on the planet. This might lead serendipitously to new forms of wild iris like those found growing on farms in the Mississippi Delta, or to a further proliferation of highly competitive weeds, such as the new bush honeysuckle hybrid *Lonicera* x *bella*, that will invade the few areas left relatively untouched by human disturbance, exterminating the ancient species in their path. Or we can summon up the courage to play that privileged part in the evolutionary drama for which we, the most aware and most self-conscious of all nature's creations, seem destined.

I believe that for now, our primary responsibility is to be the preservers and restorers of those native species and communities that are the glorious incarnation of three and a half billion years' worth of nature's creativity. How can we, in good conscience, let them slip away before our very eyes? But we should also be free to experiment, to let our imaginations run wild, to learn how to be the creators of biodiversity as well as its preservers and restorers. Someday, thanks to John Todd and other pioneers, we'll know enough about ecology to be able to develop new plant communities, combining species from around the globe, that add to, rather than subtract from, Earth's wonderful diversity of life forms. Even as we compensate for water pollution and the other disturbances we cause to the land we live on, we'll be creating totally new and ecologically rich garden habitats—taking the next great evolutionary leap in the dazzling history of landscape design.

The Garden of Ashes

WHEN PEOPLE THINK of Brooklyn, they generally think of cannolis or knishes. But plants? When I moved to Brooklyn, everyone thought I was going out of my mind. Brooklyn is the despoiled Eden that most Americans have spent their lives trying to get away from—among them my mom, who was born not far from the site where Henry Hudson first landed on Long Island, and who left for the suburbs at the age of twenty-six. People really think I'm off my rocker when I say that, for me, a small, green oasis amid Brooklyn's concrete and brick has become a model for the future of the garden: the Brooklyn Botanic Garden, where I work.

The Brooklyn Botanic Garden (or BBG) is a sort of floristic record of our evolving perceptions of nature and how we fit into it. There's something soothing, even Edenlike, about this most urban of gardens. The Garden of Eden, humanity's original home, is said to have been a land of perpetual spring, where Adam and Eve lived among trees that flowered and fruited continuously—a kind of southern California, but without the earthquakes. We don't have earthquakes in Brooklyn, though the ground does shudder as the subway rumbles by, and winter puts a temporary pall on all the flowering and fruiting. However, the Botanic Garden is a place where residents of one of the Earth's greatest cities have been able, throughout the twentieth century, to enter an almost sacred space and be comforted by contact with the rest of nature, and where species flourish under human care.

I'm not suggesting that BBG is a horticultural throwback to some hoary vision of paradise. At every turn in a garden path, there is a reminder that Adam and Eve ate the forbidden fruit and were thrown out of the earthly paradise into a baffling, disorderly world. In the seventeenth century, the poet Andrew Marvell described it this way:

> 'Tis not, what once it was, the world
> But a rude heap together hurl'd;
> All negligently overthrown,
> Gulfes, Deserts, Precipices, Stone . . .

We gardeners have been struggling ever since Eden to make sense of our postlapsarian landscape.

I'm sure Marvell would have approved of BBG's Herb Garden, with its knot garden, a perfectly symmetrical, sixteenth-century vision of divine perfection. Based on a design credited to Thomas Hill's *The Gardener's Labyrinth* (1577), it was installed in 1938, the year after this garden-within-the-Garden was begun with help from the Depression-era Works Progress Administration. The original knot was composed of sweet violet, lavender cotton, and thyme, with the beds on the west and south sides containing kitchen and perfumery herbs. The rest of the garden was planted with poisonous and medicinal species, reflecting the fact that the science of botany—and indeed, the very institution

The Brooklyn Botanic Garden's Herb Garden,
with an Elizabethan knot garden surrounded
by beds of culinary and medicinal plants.

of the botanic garden—derive from the desire to bring together in one place, for the convenience of study, plants that either are or might conceivably one day be used in the treatment of disease. Today, because our focus has shifted from survival to pleasure, there is a much higher proportion of culinary and flowering plants.

No less than half of BBG's fifty-two acres is devoted to the Plant Family Collection, in which various plant taxa are displayed in the order in which they evolved on Earth. Beyond the world-famous Japanese Hill-and-Pond Garden and the Cranford Rose Garden with its five thousand bushes of America's favorite flower, this systematic planting is a testament to the Age of Reason, whose dawn, in the eighteenth century, gave rise to the scientific revolutions that have shaped the modern world. At the northern end of the Plant Family Collection are ferns and, notably, conifers, the most important class of gymnosperms, those ancient cone-bearing plants whose ovules are naked, rather than enclosed in ovaries as in later species. Majestic specimens belonging to the Cupressaceae (cypress), Pinaceae (pine), Taxaceae (yew), and other families gradually give way to the Magnoliaceae (magnolia), the Nymphaeaceae (water-lily), and other representatives of the great phylum of angiosperms, the flowering plants that appeared in the mid-Cretaceous period, only moments ago in evolutionary time. Within a mere five million years, the angiosperms, with the assistance of the insects and other animals that pollinated their flowers and dispersed their seeds, would come to dominate the world.

BBG's Rock Garden, the first of its kind in an American botanic garden, was created in the early decades of this century, when horticultural tastemakers were rebelling against the stifling artifice of Victorian landscapes and looking to wild nature for inspiration. Conceived at a time when anything even remotely resembling the typical Victorian garden had these tastemakers foaming at the mouth, the rock garden, which alludes to the utterly wild realm of alpine meadows and rock-strewn slopes found on the Earth's most magnificent mountains, is the very antithesis of the Victorian carpet bed. Seventy or eighty years ago, rock gardening was popular but far from perfected. In a 1934 book written on the subject for *McCalls* magazine, Brooklyn Botanic Garden horticulturist Montague Free grumbled about the "rockeries" that erupted from the center of so many American lawns "like Gargantuan hot-cross buns, lavishly spotted with raisins." By contrast, BBG's rock garden was an artless rendition of the kind of vegetation that might be found amid natural glacial scree. The boulders that are this garden's bones were assembled mostly from the site itself, which crowns the moraine dumped by the last glacier as it retreated northward from Long Island more than ten thousand years ago.

The Native Flora Garden, one of the world's first ecological gardens, harbors plants native to the New York metropolitan region, from golden-club, a member of the arum family with yellow flowering spikes that rise above the water of the kettle pond in May, to tupelo, which initiates the autumn foliage spectacle with a scarlet blaze. This wild retreat—begun in 1911, when the word *ecology* had yet to enter the popular lexicon—comprises eight plant communities native to an area known for its natural diversity. Included here are a serpentine area, dry and wet meadows, a bog, pine barrens, an oak forest, and a limestone ledge.

Yet for me, what is most truly inspirational about the Brooklyn Botanic Garden is not just its veritable archive of Western garden design, nor its exquisite textures and colors and fragrances. It's the fact that the entire place was created from a turn-of-the-century ash heap. This former waste dump is a symbol of the kind of ecological transformation that may be effected in our own backyards and beyond if only we will plunge our hands into the soil, heal the long-ruptured link between nature and daily life, and restore human nature to its rightful place in the larger ecological community.

Golden club (Orontium aquaticum)
in the Brooklyn Botanic Garden's Native Flora Garden.

A FEW YEARS ago, I went to a retirement party. An engineer who worked with my husband, Don, was leaving his job after dedicating a lifetime to designing bits and pieces of New York City's infrastructure. Clancy and I had never met before, but he'd heard that I'd written an environmental book, and he must have been expecting some tree-hugging radical. No sooner did we shake hands than he said, "Janet, you know, the best environmentalist is not a banner-waving protester. The best environmentalist is an engineer who believes in God."

Now, anyone who can calculate the stress load on every single cable of the Brooklyn Bridge seems like a rocket scientist to me, but still, I had to respectfully disagree with Clancy on this point. I'm convinced that the environmental heroes of the twenty-first century will in fact be humble gardeners—gardeners who believe that it is their responsibility, maybe even their destiny, to promote a richer evolution of life on Earth through a new, ecologically wise landscape art.

Scientists predict that the biodiversity crisis will reach a crescendo sometime during the first half of the next century. Changes with great ecological and genetic import for both plants and animals are anticipated within the next twenty to fifty years due to global warming alone. Fortunately, there seems to be a growing international consensus on the need to reduce the emissions of carbon dioxide and other gases, which may already be altering the Earth's climate. Meanwhile, conservation biologists are beginning to piece together a picture of what the Earth's landscape will have to look like in the coming decades if we are to stem the rising tide of extinction. It must be a lot like the Brooklyn Botanic Garden writ large—an assemblage of gardens within the global garden.

The new planetary landscape will revolve around large, unobtrusively managed "wild" reserves, representing the best remaining examples of ancient and unique ecosystems. These biological gardens—"gardens" because they could not survive without active restoration efforts by humans—will be designed to ensure the continuing evolution of the myriad plants and animals with which we evolved. The ideal size for each reserve will depend on the particular needs of its top predator species. In "The Biogeography of the Mega-zoo," Arthur Sullivan and Mark Shaffer estimate that the minimum size for such reserves must be about 600 to 750 square kilometers. The Sierra Club calculates that wild lands of at least four thousand square kilometers will be necessary to accommodate viable populations of all species.

According to the Organization for Economic Cooperation and Development, in 1990 there were 5,289 protected areas in the world, comprising a total of some 5.3 million square kilometers, or about 4 percent of the Earth's surface. Many biologists set 10 percent as a target figure for protection. Although the total area in reserves has grown by more than 700 percent since 1950 and 300 percent since 1970, it remains to be seen whether 10 percent is an achievable goal, at least in a world in which the human population has not yet stabilized.

The United Nations has already put in place the skeleton of a global reserve system as part of UNESCO's Man and the Biosphere program. A protected natural area is at the core of the typical biosphere reserve. Surrounding this wild core is a zone of landscape that is managed more intensively but still in an ecologically sensitive way—for example, used for farming, fishing, grazing, or recreation. With more than three hundred biosphere reserves in seventy-five countries—forty-seven of them in the United States alone, from the New Jersey pinelands to the Everglades to Yellowstone—the UNESCO program already constitutes a truly global framework in which humans and the rest of nature can coevolve. UNESCO hopes eventually to have biosphere reserves in all of the 193 areas around the globe that have been designated as biogeographical provinces by the World

Conservation Union (formerly called the International Union for the Conservation of Nature).

In places where the natural landscape has been utterly fragmented and large tracts of wild landscape no longer exist, natural communities will have to be restored. The science of restoration ecology—essentially gardening on a grand scale—is teaching us how to put the pieces back together, how to restore natural processes so that nature can heal itself and get on with the business of evolution.

Some areas are logical candidates for intensive restoration efforts—for example, the second-growth forests of the eastern United States. Although many forests are now returning, some two centuries after being cleared by colonists for agriculture, forest fragmentation is nonetheless occurring over large portions of the East, according to a recent study by James Vogelmann of the University of New Hampshire. Human activities, especially residential development and its associated roads, are dissecting large and contiguous swaths of regenerating forest. In much of the area of southern New England that he focused on, which included 157 townships in southern New Hampshire and northeastern Massachusetts, Vogelmann found that forest fragmentation had increased over the past two decades. He also discovered that most fragmentation took place during the very first stages of population growth—in other words, on the expanding urban fringe. He believes that his findings are applicable across a large part of the eastern region. Studies such as this should prove very useful in flagging areas that are a high priority for restoration and at the same time particularly vulnerable to fragmentation due to suburban development.

In the Great Plains, the problem is not surging development but rather agriculture, which has become ever more marginal in recent decades. Here, rainfall teeters on the brink of inadequacy for crop production. Agriculture as it's currently practiced can be maintained only by pumping water from the immense Ogallalah aquifer, and water tables are dropping. Recognizing that the days of water-intensive agriculture are numbered, two social scientists, Frank and Deborah Popper, have proposed a huge restoration project for the region, to be called the Buffalo Commons. Under their plan, much of the landscape would be returned to the bison that once grazed the shortgrass prairies growing naturally in the Plains states. The Buffalo Commons would encompass a vast area of grassy plains extending from northern Texas to southern Canada. Buffalo ranching is in fact already beginning to catch on in the northern plains, whose harsh climate makes conventional cattle ranching as well as crop production problematic.

Ecologists have yet to figure out how to restore many degraded ecosystems. In the United States alone, these include the longleaf pine–wiregass community of the South, which has been destroyed by forestry; the overgrazed sagebrush steppe in the intermountain region of the West, where native perennial grasses have been replaced by cheatgrass; and the spruce-fir forests of the southern Appalachians, where air pollution and the introduced balsam woolly adelgid have virtually eliminated mature stands. Then, too, there are those natural communities of which no viable examples remain, such as the Black Belt prairies of Alabama and Mississippi, the bluegrass savanna–woodland of Kentucky, the canebrakes of the South, and the alkali sink scrub of the southern San Joaquin Valley in California.

Some of the first restorations undertaken have met with only mixed success. After sixty years, the restored prairie at the University of Wisconsin–Madison Arboretum is still lacking many species native to its pre-European tallgrass ancestor, and non-native weeds pose a persistent problem. What's more, all such attempts to date at ecological restoration have been on a relatively small scale, and therefore are limited in their ability to produce new evolutionary mutations and adaptations. In the end, the best way to succeed in restoring ecosystems is to continue trying to re-create them.

Natural reserves, whether preserved or restored, will be of little value if they remain cut off from one another. A paper on the flora of Staten Island published in the *Bulletin of the Torrey Botanical Club*, which documented losses of 40 percent of the native plant species over the past century—and this on an island on which some 10 percent of the land is protected, twice the national percentage—suggests that even the common conservation target of 10 percent may be far too low if the rest of the landscape is allowed to be tattered by urban and suburban development. In a recent paper in the journal *Conservation Biology*, William Newmark of the University of California at San Diego came to a similar conclusion concerning national parks located in the Rocky Mountains, in the Sierra-Cascades, and on the Colorado Plateau. Newmark found that the number of extinctions of mammals in parks such as Yosemite, Yellowstone, Jasper, and Banff exceeded the number of colonizations—in other words, the animals are well on their way to extirpation, even in an area of North America that is relatively well endowed with wilderness. Since the parks were first established, twenty-nine populations of mammals have become extinct, including not only large mammals such as the gray wolf, elk, and caribou but also smaller species such as the white-tailed jackrabbit and the spotted skunk. This is not good news, if only because such natural reserves will most likely be the final repository of many of the world's creatures in the next century, given current global rates of human population growth and accompanying habitat loss.

The reserves will have to be connected by green corridors, to serve as avenues for animal migration and seed dispersal as well as for the movement of genes both within and among populations of organisms. By means of such land bridges, we may be able to transform an archipelago of lonely islands of wilderness into a functional unit big enough to provide for the integrity of entire biomes. These green corridors will be particularly critical in times of climate change, when organisms will have to move at rates never before seen in the fossil record in order to keep pace with shifting habitat conditions—just to survive.

Again, conservation biologists are only now beginning to figure out how the size and shape as well as the location of such natural corridors will affect their ability to safeguard individual species and whole ecologies. They suspect that a network of different kinds of corridors will be needed to ensure diversity. Fencerows and wild gardens in residential areas will enable small mammals such as white-footed mice and chipmunks, many birds and pollinators, and amphibians to move across the landscape. Larger movement corridors will be required to enable wide-ranging animals such as bears and mountain lions to meet their daily needs for food, water, and shelter, and to allow the seasonal migrations of other species such as caribou and elk. Still larger corridors, encompassing the entire range of topography and habitat in a landscape, from river to ridgetop, will be necessary to preserve large-scale ecological processes. Reed Noss and Larry Harris, two of the leading proponents of landscape linkages, point out, for example, that the unique herb-bog communities of the Gulf coastal plain, with their extremely diverse vegetation, would be destroyed were it not for the broad corridors that allow fires in upland pinelands to sweep down and prune back the wetland shrubs that would otherwise encroach on them.

Just as important as the need to connect wildlands, however, is the need to protect them from the invasive weeds that are another principal cause of their demise. But the anti-human ideology that infects much environmentalism is not necessary to rationalize this; indeed, we should be preserving for study not only the remaining wilderness areas but also the most disturbed habitats of our own creation—from roadsides and pastures to mine spoils and waste dumps—and searching them for signs of new hybrids or other resilient life forms that may be instrumental in the restoration of even these most ravaged of landscapes.

In fact, in the twenty-first century, the diversity of life will depend on a whole continuum of landscapes, from the fully wild to the fully domesticated. Outside the wild reserves, permacultures and organic farms will grow diverse crops of heirloom varieties and modern hybrids—the fruits of our traditional efforts to enrich plant life—to nourish nearby human population centers. Biodiverse gardens in the suburbs will provide living space for people as well as a surprisingly large number of plant and animal species.

Metropolitan areas will continue to spread, at least until the human population stabilizes, but in a way that will embrace and complement the regional ecology instead of obliterating it. All the gardens-within-the-garden that first evolved in the residential landscape—the kitchen garden, the wild garden, the water garden, and the rest—will now, on a larger scale, define the regional landscape as well.

"Under every city," according to John and Nancy Todd, "there is a dark and hidden Venice," a labyrinthine system of pipes and culverts that delivers clean water efficiently but dumps polluted effluent into the last remaining natural waterways. Like the real Venice, cities of the future will celebrate natural water cycles for all to see. In smaller urban areas, both sewage and the tainted runoff from roofs and streets will be purified in man-made ponds and wetlands, where plants and microorganisms will assimilate nutrients and other pollutants and recycle them through the landscape. In more densely populated cities, Living Machines—perhaps designed as long, thin, greenhouselike structures running along the streets, doubling as barriers to protect pedestrians from traffic—will employ a variety of plants and microorganisms to turn sewage and runoff into purified water.

Even in the inner city, tentacles of urban wildness will provide habitat for beleaguered urban wildlife and venues for hiking, birdwatching, and other kinds of human recreation. They'll also help filter polluted air and, by creating cooling breezes, moderate the heat-island effect that makes cities so much warmer than surrounding areas.

A more domesticated kind of gardening will also thrive in the ecological city. Urban areas have the potential to produce a great deal of their own food, whether in vacant lots transformed into community gardens, in abandoned warehouses converted into indoor agricultural enterprises, or on rooftops and in traditional backyards.

FOR MILLIONS OF years, birds and bees have been the agents of biodiversity, scattering seed and pollen across the land. Now we humans will have to play a similar role.

During much of the history of life on Earth, our ancestors evolved biologically. This mostly plodding, incremental process of change, encoded in the genes, drove evolution for thousands and thousands of generations. For the comparatively brief period of human history, by contrast, evolution has occurred primarily by means of *cultural* change, through the development of language, the invention of primitive tools, and the creation of agriculture, cities, and advanced technology. Cultural evolution, a process of change in behavior that can happen within a decade or less and then be passed down through imitation and learning from generation to generation, is now subsuming the far slower process of biological evolution.

It has been only a few hundred generations since the Agricultural Revolution, when humans undertook the radical redesign of the terrestrial landscape. It's been only about ten generations since we began, during the Industrial Revolution, to tamper with the planet's very biogeochemistry. Because our scientific and moral understanding has not yet caught up with these breathtaking technological developments, the negative as well as the positive consequences have been profound. And so we find ourselves grappling with the frightening prospect of radical climate change and mass extinction.

Neurobiologists tell us that our nervous system evolved in response to a vastly different world. The human gene pool, via biological evolution, cannot change fast enough to enable a species originally designed to respond to immediate danger—the cracking of a branch, say, signaling the approach of a predator—to grasp the enormity of problems that seem by comparison to be proceeding in slow motion, such as global warming or the extinction crisis. However, our new technologies are enabling us, at least to some extent, to anticipate adverse environmental changes, and therefore affording us the opportunity to change our behavior to compensate for them. Information technologies invented for the purposes of spying and perfecting the accuracy of deadly modern weapons, for example, have also resulted in what one environmental analyst has called a "rudimentary planetary nervous system . . . a literal wiring of the Earth." These same technologies are now beginning to be used for mapping ecosystem changes on a regional or a continental scale, and for measuring the depletion of protective ozone in the atmosphere.

Dr. James Lovelock, author of the Gaia hypothesis—the theory that proposes that all living matter, as well as the air, the oceans, and the land, comprise parts of a giant system capable of maintaining conditions optimal for the survival of life—has also posed the next logical question: if the Earth indeed is essentially one big, self-regulating "organism," then to what extent do we humans constitute a Gaian nervous system and a brain?

A handful of other contemporary thinkers also have come to terms with the fact that we—all the intelligent species of the universe, as the most sensitive, and most aware of its parts—increasingly exert control over the whole of creation. The poet and philosopher Frederick Turner has written that the incipient nervous system represented by our technologies and our brains is like the nervous system of an unborn child. We stand at the first trembling moment of the history of the universe, the flash of a dawn which is a mere twelve billion years old, the dawn of a ten-trillion-year day. The universe is still only in its gestation; it is not yet fully developed. It is partly up to us to complete that development, to increase the awareness and control we have over the rest of the universe, to extend the nerves of science and art into the inanimate and insentient parts of the world.

The restoration ecologist William R. Jordan III has suggested that this "radical evolutionary metamorphosis"—the transcription of genetic information from its classic biological form into a new mental and cultural form—is already under way. It is enabling the biosphere, caught up as it is in the dizzying spiral of cultural evolution, to acquire "an alternative mode of reproduction" via new technologies such as restoration ecology.

In other words, we are moving toward a new evolutionary process, a process of *conscious* evolution, in which humans will shepherd the future of life on Earth.

Some writers have greeted this prospect with despair. In *The End of Nature*, Bill McKibben concludes that nature as a separate and wild province, a world apart from man, is dead. According to McKibben, we have deprived nature of its independence. Without independence, nature has no meaning; and without it, there is nothing but us.

However, it is this very perception of nature as a separate province, apart from the human realm, that has freed us to follow our own designs, paying little heed to the consequences we visit upon other creatures and natural communities. Rediscovering the underlying unity of life and our place in it, it seems to me, is the best way to try to ensure that nature as we know it will endure.

A species in possession of such enormous power cannot be

bereft of a moral compass extending the boundaries of compassion to the whole natural world. Over thousands of years, the human species has expanded the "circle of altruism," as philosophers call it, from the family and the tribe to the nation and the race and thence to all human beings. This is one of our most glorious achievements. Now we are beginning to realize that many of our most cherished activities—gardening included—are inflicting large-scale suffering on other creatures, and even leading countless numbers of them to the brink of extinction. The circle of compassion needs to be widened to embrace all of the species with which we inhabit the Earth.

Absolute equality among humans and other plant and animal species is impossible, of course. Like all animals, we must exploit and even kill other organisms in order to survive. But we should not cause unnecessary suffering or kill indiscriminately, whether intentionally or through neglect. And we certainly should not snuff out the life of entire species or ancient natural communities for all time.

And so, as great gardeners have always done, we must reinvent our relationship with the rest of nature in a fertile, creative, and playful way. Not only our own backyards but also the entire globe must become our garden. Together, the art of landscape design and the science of ecology can remake the surface of the planet. The goal of this new landscape art will be nothing less than the enhancement of the beauty and complexity of the universe through the nurturing of a greater richness and variety of earthly life.

Acknowledgments

I ran into Steve Clemants my first day on the job at the Brooklyn Botanic Garden. There are all kinds of world-class characters at an institution such as BBG—from plantsmen who scour the Earth for variegated canna cultivars to botanists who teeter off precipices of remote mountains in the Ukraine in pursuit of rare anemones. As soon as I met Steve, a mellow Minnesotan with a love of urban botany and chenopods, an obscure group of mostly ugly plants, I knew that we were kindred spirits. This book was sparked by our trek along the ocean beaches of eastern Long Island in search of the gravely threatened seabeach amaranth, the subject of the first chapter, and both Steve's infectious curiosity about what makes plants tick and his respect for the creatures with which we share this incredibly beautiful planet have been a continuing source of inspiration. Other scientists have also had a profound effect on my thinking, especially George Robinson, John Randall, Jim Luken, John Todd, and Bill Jordan. They've all confirmed my esteem for science as a noble enterprise.

I first met my editor, Ray Roberts, at lunch at a Manhattan restaurant some six years ago. It took barely two sips of wine before I was won over, and I'm still a big admirer of Ray's professionalism and his charm. I can't thank him enough for championing my work. I'm grateful, too, to others at Holt for their efforts on behalf of this book, including Niall Dunne, Dorothy Straight, John Candell, Gretchen Achilles, Paula Szafranski, Eva Diaz, and Kathleen Fridella. It is people such as these that restore my faith in publishing as a noble enterprise.

These pages are graced with Stephen Tim's exquisite botanical drawings. I owe a great debt to Steve not only as an illustrator but also as Vice President for Science at the Brooklyn Botanic Garden (and my boss). I am very fortunate that both he and Judy Zuk, President of BBG, have, over the years, trusted my instincts—even when they have led me into uncharted waters.

During the course of writing a book there are inevitably gusts and squalls. As always, my husband, Don, has helped keep me on an even keel. This book is dedicated to Don, for his sweet indulgence as well as his sturdy back.

Working for the past eight years at the Brooklyn Botanic Garden has been a great privilege. I can't imagine a better place from which to contemplate the glorious history of gardening—and from which to envision its next great evolutionary leap.

Selected Bibliography

INTRODUCTION: STALKING THE WILD AMARANTH

Adams, W. H. *Nature Perfected: Gardens through History.* New York: Abbeville Press, 1991.

Berry, B. J. L. "Urbanization." In *The Earth as Transformed by Human Action: Global and Regional Changes in the Biosphere Over the Past 300 Years,* edited by B. L. Turner II et at., 103–121. Cambridge: Cambridge University Press, 1990.

Britton, N. *Catalogue of Plants Found in New Jersey: Final Report of the State Geologist.* Vol. 2. Trenton, N.J., 1889.

Clemants, S. "New York Metropolitan Flora: Preliminary Checklist." *Contributions from the Brooklyn Botanic Garden Herbarium* 1 (1990):1–61.

Clemants, S., and C. Mangels. *Amaranthus pumilus: 1990 New York State Status Survey.* Report to the U.S. Fish and Wildlife Service. Newton Corner, Mass., 1990.

Cole, J. N. *Amaranth: From the Past for the Future.* Emmaus, Pa.: Rodale Press, 1979.

Eldredge, N. *The Miner's Canary: Unraveling the Mysteries of Extinction*. Princeton, N.J.: Princeton University Press, 1991.

Greller, A. M. "Observations on the Forests of Northern Queens County, Long Island, from Colonial Times to the Present." *Bulletin of the Torrey Botanical Club* 49, no. 4 (1972): 202–206.

Heywood, V. H., ed. *Global Biodiversity Assessment*. New York: published for the United Nations Environment Program by Cambridge University Press, 1995.

Kellert, S. R., and E. O. Wilson, eds. *The Biophilia Hypothesis*. Washington, D.C.: Island Press/Shearwater Books, 1993.

Lawton, J. H., and R. M. May. *Extinction Rates*. New York: Oxford University Press, 1995.

MacPhee, R. "The 40,000-Year Plague: A Natural History of Human-induced Extinctions." Paper presented at The Living Planet in Crisis: Biodiversity Science and Policy, a conference organized by the American Museum of Natural History Center for Biodiversity and Conservation, New York City, March 9 and 10, 1995.

Mangels, C. "Seabeach Amaranth in New York State." *New York Flora Association Newsletter* 2, no. 2 (1991): 7–8.

Marinelli, J. "Stalking the Wild Amaranth." *Plants & Gardens News* 8(1):1, 14–15.

———. "What Is a Biodiverse Garden?" In *Going Native: Biodiversity in Our Own Backyards*, edited by J. Marinelli. Brooklyn: Brooklyn Botanic Garden, 1994.

Miller, J. E., Jr., ed. *Complete Poetry and Selected Prose by Walt Whitman*. Boston: Houghton Mifflin Company, 1959.

Rafinesque, C. S. "Essential Generic and Specific Characters of Some New Genuses and Species of Plants Observed in the United States of America in 1803 and 1804." *The Medical Repository* 2, no. 5 (1808): 356–363.

Robinson, G. R., M. E. Yurlina, and S. N. Handel. "A Century of Change in the Staten Island Flora: Ecological Correlates of Species Losses and Invasions." *Bulletin of the Torrey Botanical Club* 12, no. 2 (1994): 119–129.

Sauer, J. D. "The Grain Amaranths and Their Relatives: A Revised Taxonomic and Geographic Survey." *Annals of the Missouri Botanical Garden*. 54 (1967): 103–137.

Stone, W. "The Plants of Southern New Jersey, with Especial Reference to the Flora of the Pine Barrens and the Geographic Distribution of the Species." Annual Report of the New Jersey State Museum. Trenton, N.J., 1911.

Stork, N. "The Magnitude of Global Biodiversity and Its Decline." Paper presented at The Living Planet in Crisis: Biodiversity Science and Policy, a conference organized by the American Museum of Natural History Center for Biodiversity and Conservation, New York City, March 9 and 10, 1995.

Svensen, H. K. "The Early Vegetation of Long Island." *Brooklyn Botanic Garden Record* 25, no. 3 (1936): 207–227.

Tarr, J. A. and R. U. Ayres. "The Hudson-Raritan Basin." In *The Earth as Transformed by Human Action: Global and Regional Changes in the Biosphere Over the Past 300 Years*, edited by B. L. Turner II et al., 623–629. Cambridge: Cambridge University Press, 1990.

Taylor, N. "The Vegetation of Montauk: A Study of Grassland and Forest." *Brooklyn Botanic Garden Memoirs* 2, part 1 (1923).

Turner, B. L. II, et al., eds. *The Earth as Transformed by Human Action: Global and Regional Changes in the Biosphere Over the Past 300 Years*. Cambridge: Cambridge University Press, 1990.

Weakley, A., M. Bucher, and N. Murdock. *Technical Agency Draft Recovery Plan for Seabeach Amaranth (Amaranthus pumilus Rafinesque)*. Asheville, N.C.: U.S. Department of Interior Fish and Wildlife Service Asheville Field Office, 1995.

Wilson, E. O. *The Diversity of Life*. New York: W.W. Norton & Company, 1992.

Young, S. M., ed. *New York Rare Plant Status List*. Latham, N.Y.: New York Natural Heritage Program, 1996.

GARDEN PLACE

Beecher, C. E. *A Treatise on Domestic Economy*. Boston: Marsh, Capen, Lyon, and Webb, 1847.

Beecher, C. E., and H. B. Stowe. *The American Woman's Home*. New York: J. B. Ford and Company, 1869.

Bormann, F. H., D. Balmori, and G. T. Geballe. *Redesigning the American Lawn*. New Haven: Yale University Press, 1993.

Hunt, J. D., and P. Willis. *The Genius of the Place: The English Landscape Garden 1620–1820*. New York: Harper & Row, 1975.

Jackson, K. T. *Crabgrass Frontier: The Suburbanization of the United States*. New York: Oxford University Press, 1985.

Marinelli, J. "Weather—And What to Plant." *Plants & Gardens News* 6, no. 1 (1991): 1, 10–11.

Murphy, R. K. *Fish-Shape Paumanok: Nature and Man on Long Island*. Reprint of essays prepared for a series of lectures in 1962. Great Falls, Va.: Waterline Books, 1992.

Rugoff, M. *The Beechers: An American Family in the 19th Century*. New York: Harper & Row, 1981.

Sklar, K. K. *Catharine Beecher: A Study in American Domesticity*. New Haven: Yale University Press, 1973.

Svensen, H. K. "The Early Vegetation of Long Island." *Brooklyn Botanic Garden Record* 25, no. 3 (1936): 207–227.

ALIENS, CLONES, AND THE ORIGIN OF SPECIES

Barrett, S. C. H., and J. R. Kohn. "Genetic and Evolutionary Consequences of Small Population Size in Plants: Implications for Conservation." In *Genetics and Conservation of Rare Plants*, edited by D. A. Falk and K. E. Holsinger, 3–30. New York: Oxford University Press, 1991.

Bell, A. D. *Plant Form: An Illustrated Guide to Flowering Plant Morphology*. Oxford: Oxford University Press, 1991.

Darwin, C. *The Different Forms of Flowers on Plants of the Same Species*. Chicago: University of Chicago Press, 1877.

Ehrlich, P., and A. Ehrlich. *Extinction: The Causes and Consequences of the Disappearance of Species*. New York: Random House, 1981.

Falk, D. A., and K. E. Holsinger, eds. *Genetics and Conservation of Rare Plants*. New York: Oxford University Press, 1991.

Frankel, O. H., A. H. D. Brown, and J. J. Burdon. *The Conservation of Plant Diversity*. Cambridge: Cambridge University Press, 1995.

Hamrick, J. L., M. J. W. Godt, D. A. Murawski, and M. D. Loveless. "Correlations Between Species Traits and Allozyme Diversity: Implications for Conservation Biology." In *Genetics and Conservation of Rare Plants*, edited by D. A. Falk and K. E. Holsinger, 75–86. New York: Oxford University Press, 1991.

Heywood, V. H., ed. *Global Biodiversity Assessment*. New York: published for the United Nations Environment Program by Cambridge University Press, 1995.

J. L. Hudson, Seedsman. "Natives vs. Exotics: The Myth of the Menace." In the 1994 Ethnobotanical Catalog of Seeds, 92. Redwood City, Calif.

Huenneke, L. F. "Ecological Implications of Genetic Variation in Plant Populations." In *Genetics and Conservation of Rare Plants*, edited by D. A. Falk and K. E. Holsinger, 31–44. New York: Oxford University Press, 1991.

Luken, J. O. "Valuing Plants in Natural Areas." *Natural Areas Journal* 14, no. 4 (1994): 295–299.

Luken, J. O., and J. W. Thieret. "Amur Honeysuckle: Its Fall from Grace." *Bioscience* 46, no. 1 (1996): 18–24.

MacArthur, R. H., and E. O. Wilson. *The Theory of Island Biogeography.* Princeton: Princeton University Press, 1967.

Marinelli, J. "Native or Not?" *Plants & Gardens News* 10, no. 3 (1995): 1, 14–15.

———. "The Nazi Connection, Continued." *Restoration & Management Notes* 13, no. 2 (1995): 179–182.

Menges, E. S. "The Application of Minimum Viable Population Theory to Plants." In *Genetics and Conservation of Rare Plants*, edited by D. A. Falk and K. E. Holsinger, 45–61. New York: Oxford University Press, 1991.

Millar, C. I., and W. J. Libby. "Strategies for Conserving Clinal, Ecotypic, and Disjunct Population Diversity in Widespread Species." In *Genetics and Conservation of Rare Plants*, edited by D. A. Falk and K. E. Holsinger, 149–170. New York: Oxford University Press, 1991.

Randall, J. M., and J. Marinelli, eds. *Invasive Plants: Weeds of the Global Garden*. Brooklyn: Brooklyn Botanic Garden, 1996.

Rieseberg, L. H. "Hybridization in Rare Plants: Insights from Case Studies in *Cercocarpus* and *Helianthus*." In *Genetics and Conservation of Rare Plants*, edited by D. A. Falk and K. E. Holsinger, 171–181. New York: Oxford University Press, 1991.

Robinson, G. R., M. E. Yurlina and S. N. Handel. "A Century of Change in the Staten Island Flora: Ecological Correlates of Species Losses and Invasions." *Bulletin of the Torrey Botanical Club* 12, no. 2 (1994): 119–129.

Robinson, G. R., and J. F. Quinn. "Habitat Fragmentation, Species Diversity, Extinction, and Design of Nature Reserves." In *Applied Population Biology*, edited by S. K. Jain and L. W. Botsford, 223–248. Netherlands: Kluwer Academic Publishers, 1992.

Weberling, D. F. *Morphology of Flowers and Inflorescences*. Cambridge: Cambridge University Press, 1989.

GARDEN ANGST

Adams, W. H. *Nature Perfected: Gardens through History*. New York: Abbeville Press, 1991.

Bateson, G., *Mind and Nature: A Necessary Unity*. New York: E. P. Dutton, 1979.

Berkeley, G. *The Principles of Human Knowledge, and Three Dialogues between Hylas and Philonous*. Cleveland: World Publishing Company, 1963.

Francis, M., and R. T. Hester, Jr. *The Meaning of Gardens*. Cambridge: MIT Press, 1990.

Hume, D. *An Enquiry Concerning Human Understanding*. Buffalo: Prometheus Books, 1988.

———. *A Treatise on Human Nature*. Oxford: Clarendon Press, 1988.

Hunt, J. D., and P. Willis. *The Genius of the Place: The English Landscape Garden 1620–1820*. New York: Harper & Row, 1975.

Jekyll, G. *Colour in the Flower Garden*. 1908; reprint, Portland, Ore.: Sagapress/Timber Press, 1995.

Jellicoe, G., and S. Jellicoe. *The Landscape of Man: Shaping the Environment from Prehistory to the Present Day*. London: Thames and Hudson, 1995.

Jordan, W. R., III. "Restoration as Realization." *Restoration & Management Notes* 7, no. 1 (1989): 2.

Kern, B., and K. Kern. *The Owner-Built Homestead*. New York, Charles Scribner's Sons, 1977.

Locke, J. *An Essay Concerning Human Understanding*. Oxford: Clarendon Press, 1924.

Logsdon, G. *Two-Acre Eden*. Emmaus, Pa.: Rodale Press, 1980.

Lovelock, J. E. *Gaia: A New Look at Life on Earth*. Oxford: Oxford University Press, 1979.

Plato. *Protagoras and Meno*. Baltimore: Penguin Books, 1956.

———. *Republic*. Cambridge: Cambridge University Press, 1966.

Plumtre, G. *The Garden Makers: The Great Tradition of Garden Design from 1600 to the Present Day*. New York: Random House, 1993.

Punch, W. T., ed. *Keeping Eden: A History of Gardening in America*. Boston: Bulfinch Press/Little, Brown, 1992.

Robinson, W. *The English Flower Garden*. New York: Sagapress, 1984.

———. *The Wild Garden*. Portland, Ore.: Sagapress/Timber Press, 1994.

Thacker, C. *The History of Gardens*. London: Croom Helm, 1979.

Turner, F. "The Humble Bee: Restoration as Natural Reproduction." *Restoration & Management Notes* 5, no. 1 (1987): 15–17.

———. *The Culture of Hope: A New Birth of the Classical Spirit*. New York: The Free Press, 1995.

Weiss, A. S. *Mirrors of Infinity: The French Formal Garden and 17th-Century Metaphysics*. New York: Princeton Architectural Press, 1995.

Wrede, S., and W. H. Adams, eds. *Denatured Visions: Landscape and Culture in the Twentieth Century*. New York: Museum of Modern Art, 1991.

GARDENS THAT ACT LIKE NATURE

Bormann, F. H., and G. E. Likens. "Nutrient Cycling." *Science* 155, no. 3461 (1967): 424–429.

———. *Pattern and Process in a Forested Ecosystem*. New York: Springer Verlag, 1979.

Barbour, M. G., and W. D. Billings, eds. *North American Terrestrial Vegetation*. New York: Cambridge University Press, 1988.

Barbour, M. G., J. H. Burk, and W. D. Pitts, *Terrestrial Plant Ecology*, 2d ed. Menlo Park, Calif.: Benjamin/Cummings Publishing Company, Inc., 1987.

Bahouth, Peter. Seeds of Change catalog. Santa Fe, 1994.

Clements, F. E. "Climax Formations of North America." In *Plant Succession*. Washington, D.C.: Carnegie Institute Publication 242, 1916.

———. *Plant Succession and Indicators*. New York: H. W. Wilson Co., 1928.

Flora of North America Editorial Committee. *Flora of North America North of Mexico*. New York: Oxford University Press, 1993.

Gleason, H. A., and A. Cronquist. *The Natural Geography of Plants*. New York: Columbia University Press, 1964.

Golley, F. B. *A History of the Ecosystem Concept in Ecology: More than the Sum of the Parts*. New Haven: Yale University Press, 1993.

Hartman, J. M. "Ecological Interactions in the Garden." Paper presented at What a Combination: Inspirations for Putting Plants Together, a symposium organized by the Longwood Graduate Program Symposium and the Winterthur Garden Department, Longwood Gardens, Kennett Square, Pa., March 24, 1995.

Hartman, J. M., J. F. Thorne, and C. E. Bristow. "Variations in Old Field Succession." In *Conference Proceedings of the Council of Educators in Landscape Architecture*, vol. 4. Washington, D.C.: Council of Educators in Landscape Architecture, 1992.

Larcher, W. *Physiological Plant Ecology: Ecophysiology and Stress Physiology of Functional Groups*. 3d ed. New York: Springer Verlag, 1995.

Leopold, A. *A Sand County Almanac*. New York: Oxford University Press, 1949.

Lindeman, R. L. *Ecological Dynamics in a Senescent Lake*. Ph.D. diss., University of Minnesota, 1941.

———. "The Trophic-Dynamic Aspect of Ecology." *Ecology* 23, no. 4 (1942): 399–418.

Lyle, J. T. *Regenerative Design for Sustainable Development*. New York: John Wiley & Sons, Inc., 1994.

Marinelli, J. "After the Flush." *Garbage* 2, no. 1 (1990): 24–35.

Marinelli, J., with R. Kourik. *The Naturally Elegant Home: Environmental Style*. Boston and New York: Little, Brown and Company, 1993.

Odum, E. *Fundamentals of Ecology*. Philadelphia: W. B. Saunders, 1953.

Tansley, A. G. "The Use and Abuse of Vegetation Concepts and Terms." *Ecology* 16, no. 3 (1935): 284–307.

Tivy, J. *Biogeography: A Study of Plants in the Ecosphere*. New York: John Wiley & Sons, Inc., 1993.

Todd, N. J., and J. Todd. *From Eco-Cities to Living Machines: Principles of Ecological Design*. Berkeley: North Atlantic Books, 1994.

Turner, F. "The Self-Effacing Art: Restoration as Imitation of Nature." In *Restoration Ecology: A Synthetic Approach to Ecological Research*, edited by W. R. Jordan III, M. E. Gilpin, and J. D. Aber, 47–51. New York: Cambridge University Press, 1987.

Van der Ryn, S., and S. Cowan. *Ecological Design*. Washington, D.C.: Island Press, 1996.

Weaver, J. E., and F. E. Clements. *Plant Ecology*. New York: McGraw-Hill, 1929.

Weinstein, G. "A Biodiverse Garden for Colorado." In *Going Native: Biodiversity in Our Own Backyards*, edited by J. Marinelli. Brooklyn: Brooklyn Botanic Garden, 1994.

Wright, F. L. *The Natural House*. New York: Horizon Press, 1954.

GARDENS WITHIN THE GARDEN

Altieri, M. *Biodiversity and Pest Management in Agroecosystems*. Binghamton, N.Y.: Hayworth Press, Inc., 1994.

Barbour, M. G., J. H. Burk, and W. D. Pitts. *Terrestrial Plant Ecology*. Menlo Park, Calif.: Benjamin/Cummings Publishing Company, Inc., 1987.

Beardsley, J. *Earthworks and Beyond: Contemporary Art in the Landscape*. New York: Abbeville Press, 1984.

Burrell, C. C. "Out in Front: Redesigning the American Front Yard." *Plants & Gardens News* 10, no. 2 (1995): 1, 14–15.

Campbell, S. *Let It Rot! The Gardener's Guide to Composting*. Pownall, Vt.: Storey Publishing, 1990.

Downing, A. J. *The Architecture of Country Houses*. 1850; reprint, New York: Dover, 1969.

———. *Landscape Gardening and Rural Architecture*. 1865; reprint, New York: Dover, 1991.

———. *A Treatise on the Theory and Practice of Landscape Gardening, Fourth Edition*. 4th ed., 1850; reprint, Washington, D.C.: Dumbarton Oaks, 1991.

Frankel, O. H., A. H. D. Brown, and J. J. Burdon. *The Conservation of Plant Diversity*. Cambridge: Cambridge University Press, 1995.

Heywood, V. H., ed. *Global Biodiversity Assessment*. New York: published for the United Nations Environment Program by Cambridge University Press, 1995.

Jackson, W. *New Roots for Agriculture*. Lincoln, Nebr.: University of Nebraska Press, 1980.

Jeavons, J. *How to Grow More Vegetables than You Ever Thought Possible on Less Land than You Can Imagine*. Berkeley: Ten Speed Press, 1974.

Lyle, J. T. *Regenerative Design for Sustainable Development*. New York: John Wiley & Sons, Inc., 1994.

Marinelli, J., with R. Kourik. *The Naturally Elegant Home: Environmental Style*. Boston and New York: Little, Brown and Company, 1993.

Marinelli, J., and P. Bierman-Lytle. *Your Natural Home*. Boston and New York: Little, Brown and Company, 1995.

Mollison, B. *Permaculture Two: Practical Design for Town and Country in Permanent Agriculture*. Tasmania: Tagari Books, 1979.

Mollison, B., and D. Holmgren. *Permaculture One: A Perennial Agriculture for Human Settlements*. Maryborough, Victoria, Australia: Transworld Publishers, 1978.

Nassauer, J. I. "The Aesthetics of Horticulture: Neatness as a Form of Care." *HortScience* 23, no. 6 (1988): 973–977.

———. "The Appearance of Ecological Systems as a Matter of Policy." *Landscape Ecology* 6, no. 4 (1992): 239–250.

———. "Ecological Function and the Perception of Suburban Residential Landscapes." In *Managing Urban and High-rise Recreation Settings*, edited by P. H. Gobster. St. Paul: USDA Forest Service North Central Forest Experiment Station, 1993.

———. "Messy Ecosystems, Orderly Frames." *Landscape Journal* 14, no. 2 (1995): 161–170.

Thayer, R. L., Jr. "The Experience of Sustainable Landscapes." *Landscape Journal* 8, no. 1 (1989): 101–110.

Todd, N. J., and J. Todd. *From Eco-Cities to Living Machines: Principles of Ecological Design*. Berkeley: North Atlantic Books, 1994.

Rodale, J. I., and staff. *The Complete Book of Composting*. Emmaus, Pa.: Rodale Books, 1971.

Wright, F. L. *The Natural House*. New York: Horizon Press, 1954.

THE MACHINE IN THE GARDEN

Anderson, E. "Hybridization of the Habitat." *Evolution* 2 (1948): 1–9.

———. *Introgressive Hybridization*. New York: Wiley, 1949.

Anderson, E., and L. Hubricht. "Hybridization in Tradescantia III: The Evidence for Introgressive Hybridization." *American Journal of Botany* 25 (1938): 396–402.

Anderson, E., and G. L. Stebbins, Jr. "Hybridization as an Evolutionary Stimulus." *Evolution* 8 (1954): 378–388.

Barton, N. H., and G. M. Hewitt. "Analysis of Hybrid Zones." *Annual Review of Ecological Systematics* 15 (1985): 113–148.

Falk, D. A., and K. E. Holsinger, eds. *Genetics and Conservation of Rare Plants*. New York: Oxford University Press, 1991.

Fitzgerald, F. S. *The Great Gatsby*. New York: Charles Scribner's Sons, 1925.

Heiser, C. B. "Introgression Re-examined." *Botanical Review* 39 (1973): 347–366.

Jordan, W. R. "Environmental Junkpicking and the American Garden." *Restoration & Management Notes* 6, no. 2 (1988).

————. "Restoration as Realization." *Restoration & Management Notes* 7, no. 1 (1989): 2–3.

————. "Restoring the Restorationist." *Restoration & Management Notes* 7, no. 2 (1989): 55.

————. "A New Paradigm." *Restoration & Management* Notes 9, no. 2 (1991): 64–65.

————. "The Pastoral Experiment." *Restoration & Management Notes* 9, no. 1 (1991): 2.

————. "Otro Mundo." *Restoration & Management Notes* 10, no. 1 (1992): 3.

Josephson, B. "The San Francisco Living Machine." *Annals of Earth* 13, no. 2 (1995): 11.

Josephson, B., J. Todd, S. Serfling, A. Smith, L. Stuart, and K. Locke. "1995 Report on the Performance of the Advanced Ecologically Engineered System in Frederick, Maryland." *Annals of Earth* 14, no. 1 (1996): 15–18.

Lewontin, R. C., and L. C. Birch. "Hybridization as a Source of Variation for Adaptation to New Environments." *Evolution* 20 (1966): 315–336.

Marinelli, J. "After the Flush." *Garbage* 2, no. 1 (1990): 24–35.

————. *Your Natural Home*. Boston and New York: Little, Brown and Company, 1995.

Marx, L. *The Machine in the Garden: Technology and the Pastoral Ideal in America*. New York: Oxford University Press, 1964.

Todd, J. "Living Machines." *Annals of Earth* 8, no. 1 (1990): 14–16.

Todd, J., and B. Josephson. "The Rebirth of Flax Pond." *Annals of Earth* 11, no. 3 (1993): 12–14.

————. "Living Machines: Theoretical Foundations and Design Precepts." *Annals of Earth* 12, no. 1 (1994): 16–25.

————. "Living Machines, Part Two: Theory Applied: A Mesocosm for the Treatment of Sewage." *Annals of Earth* 12, no. 2 (1994): 14–21.

————. "A Report on the Flax Pond Restoration Project." *Annals of Earth* 11, no. 3 (1994): 16–18.

————. "The Frederick, Maryland, Living Machine for Sewage Treatment: Early Performance." *Annals of Earth* 13, no. 1 (1995): 16–17.

Callicott, J. B., ed. *Companion to a Sand County Almanac: Interpretive and Critical Essays*. Madison: University of Wisconsin Press, 1987.

————. *In Defense of the Land Ethic: Essays in Environmental Philosophy*. Albany: State University of New York Press, 1989.

Ehrenfeld, D. *The Arrogance of Humanism*. New York: Oxford University Press, 1978.

Hudson, W. E., ed. *Landscape Linkages and Biodiversity*. Washington, D.C.: Island Press, 1991.

Jordan, W. R. "Restoration as Realization." *Restoration & Management Notes* 7, no. 1 (1989): 2–3.

Leopold, A. *A Sand County Almanac*. New York: Oxford University Press, 1949.

Lyle, J. T. *Regenerative Design for Sustainable Development*. New York: John Wiley & Sons, 1994.

McKibben, W. *The End of Nature*. New York: Random House, 1989.

Miller, A. S. *Gaia Connections*. Savage, Md.: Rowman & Littlefield, 1991.

Newmark, W. D. "Extinction of Mammal Populations in Western North American National Parks." *Conservation Biology* 9, no. 3 (1995): 512–526.

Noss, R. F. "The Perils of Pollyannas." *Conservation Biology* 9, no. 4 (1995): 701–703.

Orr, D. W. "Conservation and Conservatism." *Conservation Biology* 9, no. 2 (1995): 242–245.

Robinson, G. R., M. E. Yurlina, and S. N. Handel. "A Century of Change in the Staten Island Flora: Ecological Correlates of Species Losses and Invasions." *Bulletin of the Torrey Botanical Club* 12, no. 2 (1994): 119–129.

Todd, N. J., and J. Todd. *From Eco-Cities to Living Machines: Principles of Ecological Design*. Berkeley: North Atlantic Books, 1994.

Turner, F. *The Culture of Hope: A New Birth of the Classical Spirit*. New York: The Free Press, 1995.

Vogelmann, J. E. "Assessment of Forest Fragmentation in Southern New England Using Remote Sensing and Geographic Information Systems Technology." *Conservation Biology* 9, no. 2 (1995): 439–449.

Wynne-Tyson, J., ed. *The Extended Circle*. New York: Paragon House, 1989.

Index

English landscape gardens, 18, 19,
    67–68, 73, 77, 141
  drawing of, 69
Enlightenment, the, 67
Environmental Protection Agency,
    163, 170
erosion control, 57
Eskimos, 114
*Essay Concerning Human
    Understanding* (Locke), 66
Ethiopia, 162
eutrophication, 27
evapotranspiration, 168
Everglades, 88, 169
evolution, 73, 74, 137, 187, 190, 192,
    208–10
Evolution (journal), 187
extinction crisis, 1, 2, 10–11, 205,
    209, 211

faba bean *(Vicia faba)*, 151
falso indigo *(Baptisia)*, 97
Faulkner, William, 180
fertilizers, 25, 27, 105, 143, 150, 155,
    156, 158, 162
Field's Point Wastewater Treatment
    Facility, Providence, Rhode
    Island, 184, 186
Fitzgerald, F. Scott, 177–80
floodplain swamps, 170
foamflowers, 84
food chain, 79, 185
forest fragmentation, 203
Fortune, Robert, 41
fossil fuels, 25, 27, 28, 155, 162
fragmentation, habitat, 50–54, 57
Franklinia alatamaha, 129–30
Free, Montague, 199
French formal gardens, 18, 66
Fresh Kills landfill, New York, 3
front garden, 138–39, 141–48
  drawing of, 140
Fundamentals of Ecology (Odum), 80

fungicides, 150

Gaia hypothesis, 75, 208
Gaia Institute, New York, 159
Galileo, 65
Gardener's Labyrinth, The (Hill), 196
Garden Makers, The (Plumptre), 68
Garden of Eden, 195
garden room, 110–115
Geballe, Gordon, 26, 27
geranium *(Pelargonium x hortoreum
    'Mustang')*, 123, 124
gigantism, 153
glass, 119–25
Global Diversity Assessment, 10–11
global warming, 28, 50, 83, 136,
    209
globe amaranth *(Gomphrena globosa)*,
    13
golden club *(Orontium aquaticum)*,
    drawing of, 200
goldenrod *(Solidago)*, 98
Golley, Frank Benjamin, 80
grain amaranth *(Amaranthus
    hypochondriacus)*, 15
  destroyed by Cortés, 13, 16
  drawing of, 14
greasewood *(Adenostoma
    fasciculatum)*, 90
Great Basin Desert, 90
Great Gatsby, The (Fitzgerald),
    178–79
Greece, ancient, 67
green corridors, 205–6
greenhouse effect, 28
greenhouses, 70, 120, 122, 123,
    125
Green Revolution, 150
ground layer, 95
ground plum *(Astragalus)*, 97
guilds, 157, 158

habitat fragmentation, 50–54, 57